CLARE WILSON started her professional life as a red-haired 16-year-old model, rubbing shoulders with Naomi Campbell, Yasmin Le Bon and Cameron Diaz – slap bang in the middle of the '90s London fashion scene. Clare featured in many magazines and was the face of Salon Selectives, gracing TV screens as well as treading the catwalks of the world's premier fashion shows.

Originally from Somerset, Clare travelled the world on the international modelling circuit before finally settling in Bristol with her husband and three daughters. Fifteen years of modelling has equipped Clare with a wealth of energy and love for the model industry, which ultimately lead her to set up one of the most successful model agencies in the UK – Gingersnap, which she still runs today.

Clare's debut book is where her fifteen years as a top model and twenty years as an agent collide to offer a no-holds-barred peek into the secret world of modelling.

So you
want
to be a
model?

THE SECRET

LIFE OF

SUCCESSFUL

MODELS

Clare Wilson

SilverWood

Published in 2023 by SilverWood Books

SilverWood Books Ltd
14 Small Street, Bristol, BS1 1DE, United Kingdom
www.silverwoodbooks.co.uk

ISBN 978-1-80042-242-1 (paperback)

British Library Cataloguing in Publication Data
A CIP catalogue record for this book is
available from the British Library

Page design and typesetting by SilverWood Books

For Damion, Amber, Darcy and Connie,
who inspire me more than they will ever know x

Contents

Introduction

I was just fifteen when I walked into the Models 1 office for the first time. It was the middle of the summer holidays, and London was hot, vibrant and having one of its episodic moments in which – thanks to a creative explosion of youth culture; this time acid house – the capital seemed like the coolest place on earth. Models 1 headquarters was situated on the stylish King's Road in Chelsea; itself one of those trendy epicentres following the part it had played in the hippy and punk movements of yesteryear.

I still remember my sense of trepidation as I entered the building with my mum, but that was nothing compared to the shivers that came over me as I walked into the reception area, practically hiding behind her. Roxette's 'The Look' blared from the radio, but the sound that has really stayed with me is the buzz of a hectic office. It was expectant, knowing and self-assured – the exact opposite of me, in fact. As I looked around at the framed covers of *Vogue*, *Elle*, *Harpers* and *Cosmopolitan*, I caught a glimpse of my own reflection in the glass of one of them. I was a gangly, skinny, awkward red-headed girl from Somerset, with a weird, grown-out hairstyle. The idea that I fitted in here was almost laughable. Except, it turns out, I did. Just as Marie Fredriksson was singing, I did indeed have the look. But back then, I wasn't convinced. This was Models 1, for goodness sake – one of the most prestigious model agencies in the world! The agency that represented Twiggy, Jerry Hall,

Yasmin Le Bon and most of the supermodels who covered my bedroom walls. As I stood in their reception, with my bowl cut and dressed in my snow-washed jeans, I had no idea that this was my first taste of a world that would shape my career – and my life – forever.

For the next fifteen years, I worked with Models 1, gracing catwalks, covers and commercials. I travelled the world and experienced every side of the modelling industry – both the ups and the downs. From the age of twenty-five and thirty, I slowed down and had two daughters before eventually opening my very own modelling agency, Gingersnap.

I've been an agent for twenty years now, and was modelling for almost as long before that. So you can trust me. I know this industry. I know what it takes to become a model and, just as importantly, how to avoid the many pitfalls. Let's unpack the headlines and take a peek behind the stage curtain, and let me show you how to be a successful model. We're going to talk agencies, portfolios, castings, shoots, scams, social media, testing, travelling and everything in between. We will discuss all kinds of modelling: kids, fitting, male, family, fashion, commercial and plus size. My aims are to dispel the myths, shed light on the inner sanctum of the industry and answer your most pressing questions. I want to make our world more accessible for aspiring models, extras, make-up artists, agents, stylists and directors.

You should consider this book your invaluable 'how to' pocket guide. It's full of secrets and unspoken rules that took me years to understand. I've studied other models, asked ridiculous questions and, yes, made some *huge* mistakes, all so that you don't have to.

So, without further ado, step into my office! Let's take to the catwalk, and I shall walk you through this crazy, amazing and exhilarating world.

Clarey tip:

For your constant reference, Clarey's A–Z of Modelling
will give you the lowdown on every aspect of the industry
and provide a quick guide to its complicated jargon. Find
it at the back of this book.

Getting Noticed

Unfortunately, there's no secret sauce to ensure that you're discovered and/or scouted. If there was, believe me, I'd tell you. There are thousands of ways in which models could take those first tentative steps into modelling. For some lucky ones, like Kate Moss, it's a chance meeting in a departure lounge at an airport with an international agent. It could be a young model working with an assistant who turns out to be the next Mario Testino, or a slow burn like my career which started off with part-time work on teen magazines and ended with *Vogue* and huge hair campaigns.

My own experience was fairly routine – I wasn't discovered in an airport, or after winning a beauty pageant like Helena Christensen. The year was 1988, and I was a fairly regular, if slightly self-conscious, fifteen-year-old who watched *The Clothes Show* avidly every Sunday night and was interested in modelling. It was my mum who heard on the local radio station that Models 1 were coming to Bristol to scout for new models. So, one rainy Saturday, I took the short train journey from Taunton with my twin brother Alex, found the hotel where they were seeing people, and waited for my turn. Eventually, I went into a room where a panel of Models 1 staff sat behind a long table covered with tape measures and forms. As I filled in a form, the scouts stared at me with their heads tilted to one side, eyes going up and down. They asked me my age and shoe size. (I know now that shoe size generally gives some indication of height

– these days, I find myself asking new models the same question!) And so it was that, a few weeks later, they got in touch with my mum and invited us up to London for a further meeting and so that we could check out how everything worked. That was the beginning of my modelling life. See – nothing glamorous at all!

But, while you wouldn't really know it, scouts have eyes everywhere. They mainly come in the form of creative types like make-up artists, photographers, other models, shoot producers, clients and, of course, agents. As we know, the delectable Kate Moss was discovered in an airport by Sarah Doukas of Storm Models. Kate was just in the right place at the right time – and went on to become one of the most successful models in history, with a net worth (in 2022) of £70 million according to the website celebritynetworth.com. Of course, if you or your child are approached by anyone in public, take their details and go back and complete all the necessary due diligence checks. You want to make sure that the person who has scouted you is who they say they are, and that the opportunity they offer is a genuine one.

These days, a more likely place to be discovered is on social media. Model agencies spend much of their working lives on social media, scouting for models. The key to being discovered in this way, therefore, is to ensure that your socials are current, with clear, natural, unfiltered images. It's better to maintain just one vibe on your socials, like outdoorsy, fashionista, street style, party, glamorous or girl next door. I know that clients themselves search for these looks in isolation when they're hunting for potential models. So, keep posting, be current, be natural and, most importantly, be you.

A Brief History of the Modelling Industry

It all began in the second half of the nineteenth century, when the pioneering Paris-based fashion designer Charles Frederick Worth employed a young woman by the name of Marie Vernet to wear and showcase his designs at social events. This forward-thinking marketing technique is credited as the first ever modelling job. Worth and Vernet later married and became a true power couple.

Following in Worth's footsteps was Lady Lucy Duff-Gordon. After surviving the horror of the *Titanic* sinking in 1912, Duff-Gordon began to scout actresses to showcase her designs in fashion parades. With amazing foresight, she rearranged furniture and used romantic lighting to create aspirational ideas, and gave her 'live models' a part to play, with new identities characterised by grace and prestige. Her clever advertising concept paid off: clients bought into the lifestyle portrayed in her shows, and she tripled her revenue. For the first time, fashion was no longer about who you were; it was about who you *could be*. Despite these aspirational ideals, however, modelling was still considered a low-class occupation. As they used their bodies to earn a living, models were stigmatised, and the stigma was only exacerbated by the invention of the camera. Maybe this was because photographs of women encapsulated the first concepts of the 'male gaze', therefore empowering men and objectifying women. The reputation of a model was only slightly better than that of a prostitute, and the pay was probably worse.

By the 1950s, Ford Models was paving the way as one of the first – and certainly one of the most prestigious – modelling agencies in the world. Regulation of this once-surreptitious industry offered many girls the opportunity to make a career out of their hobby. The most successful models made up to $25 an hour – big bucks at the time.

Over the next decade, and alongside the advertising explosion, modelling agencies sprang up all over the world. The model was a crucial concept in the fashion world: an accessible yet aspirational public figure on catwalks, in magazines and on the burgeoning medium of television. Twiggy became the face of the Swinging Sixties, and model stories became a regular feature in magazines and newspapers. However, most models still struggled to make a steady wage.

The 1970s brought about a much-needed sea change, and, thanks to better working conditions and wages, a new independent woman emerged. In 1973 Lauren Hutton became the face of Revlon and requested a $250,000 fee – the highest-paid contract in history at the time. This was at a time when models on a shoot were paid by the hour, usually around $60. Within weeks, no girl was working by the hour. Hutton's business move had paid off – literally. She even refused to wear certain kinds of underwear on shoots, and helped direct her own image. Her Revlon campaign became a turning point in what was to become a multimillion-pound industry, with women at its very core.

The 1980s changed everything, however. This decade produced the darlings of the industry. The girls dominating the fashion world at this time – the supermodels, or 'supers':

Christy Turlington, Linda Evangelista and Naomi Campbell – were known as 'the Trinity'. Although each was famous in her own right, together they injected fresh energy into fashion. It was rare to find a corner of the industry untouched by their influence. Together they graced the cover of British *Vogue*, George Michael's music video for 'Freedom! '90', and Gianni Versace's catwalk show. They changed the industry forever. The supermodels bridged a gap between models and celebrities. Modelling had come a long way in one century. Once grossly underpaid and stigmatised, models reached a new level of fame and, according to Evangelista, probably weren't getting out of bed for less than $10,000.

After the tall, voluptuous, Amazonian figures of the Trinity – plus Cindy Crawford, Claudia Schiffer, Stephanie Seymour, Tyra Banks et al. – there followed the stick-thin aesthetic of the 1990s. Young, frail models from Eastern Europe were chewed up and spat out by the London industry, their anonymity part of their appeal. From the 'heroin chic' whirlwind of this period emerged the fourteen-year-old Kate Moss. As the golden age of the supermodel fell, little Kate from Croydon rose from the ashes of their smouldering cigarettes.

Today we find ourselves in a new age; one in which the notion of the supermodel seems increasingly outdated. In our fast-paced world of social media, it seems that dynamism and newness are key. A constant stream of 'new faces' can be found on your 'explore' page, making it doubtful that influencers and Instagram models (or, as I call them, 'instamodels') will possess staying power comparable to that of the Trinity. Despite the presence of social media supermodels such as Kendall Jenner and Gigi Hadid, it is unlikely that supermodels as we have known them in the past will serve any purpose in a world that is now defined by freshness. With every follow of a new influencer, the golden age of the supermodel becomes an ever more distant memory.

Unsurprisingly, for every picture-perfect Insta yin, there is a converse yang. These days it's commonplace to see girls – and boys – owning their insecurities as a form of backlash against the facetuned Instagram model, and these trailblazers have begun to possess unique power. From Winnie Harlow rocking her vitiligo and Ashley Graham owning her curves to Cara Delevingne changing the game with her eyebrows and Georgia May Jagger refusing to fix the gap in her teeth, these women represent a new era of the modelling industry, which is now a far kinder, more inclusive place than it ever was before. Yes, size zero models make up a chunk of the industry, but everywhere you look there are people rebelling against this standard.

My background is in fashion modelling, where everybody expects you to be a certain size. I've spent years consoling my young model friends who didn't 'make the grade'; those who were told they were too small or too fat, that their hips were too big, that their nose didn't work…it's cut-throat. I was lucky: I was always uber-thin; until I had children, that is. It was only at the tail end of my career that I experienced the rejection that my friends had suffered years before. I went to Tenerife on a catalogue job and was sent home almost immediately – I was older and larger than the model they thought they'd booked. Over the years, I had learned to love 'no' – you must as a model, for whom rejection is a part of daily life. But that was the final straw – I was devastated.

That signified the end of my modelling career and the start of a whole new chapter as an agent. At Gingersnap, we don't tell models that they should be a certain size. We don't stop models from getting crazy piercings or haircuts. I've always believed that the industry should be inclusive of all walks of life. I want you to be unapologetically who you are. The good news is that there is a place for everyone here. So come on in – let me show you around…

Be That Model

So you want to be a model? You're signed with an agency; you're a model, right? But what does it even mean to be a model? How do you act, look, speak, feel like a model? Being a model is one thing, but really *being* a model is another thing entirely. There are rules but, like with parenting, there is no rule book. Until now.

Lesson number one: a beautiful heart makes a beautiful person

Don't get me wrong, looks matter in this world, but a model is more than just a pretty face. Sure, you're going to meet people who will look at your face and your body, but your personality is much more important than you know. There are casting directors all over the country who would trade the 'perfect face' for the perfect *package*. And that's the key: you're a package, and who you are as a person is a huge part of it. The industry is jam-packed with models (even household names!) who don't fit the cookie-cutter image of 'a model'. Maybe their nose is a little big or their legs too short, but it's their personality that carries them through castings and into paid jobs. Most bookers have their favourites – models whose personalities shine through and with whom they get on. Well, guess what? Those models get booked.

Lesson number two: read the casting room

When you first enter a casting room and meet the clients, it's all about plenty of eye contact and reading the atmosphere quickly, so that you can reflect it and match the energy. But the real preparation starts well before you walk into a casting or a shoot. You need to know what you're walking into. It's imperative that you choose clothes and make-up that reflect their vibe. (Maybe don't go dressed as a sex bomb if you're going for a mum role, for example. You're eliminating yourself before you've even stepped through the door.) Make yourself relevant to them. It's really stressful running castings. The casting director is responsible for finding the right face for a brand out of hundreds of models. They don't have time to hear your life story. Castings can sometimes be over in minutes, so it's your job to convey what they want to see at first glance. The actual casting takes place quite late in the process of organising a campaign: it comes after pitches, budgeting and a *lot* of meetings. By the time you arrive in the room, they know what they are looking for. You need to make yourself what they are looking for.

Lesson number three: fail to prepare; prepare to fail

I once walked into a casting in London a little bit too confident. I'd done this hundreds of times before. I was directed into a boardroom and faced with a panel of suited and booted directors of a high-street store. They interviewed me, asking why I wanted to represent the brand. I was really taken aback. Fortunately, I had done interviews before, and they offered me the job on the spot. I had to take a few deep breaths when I got outside, though! I should've done more research about what I was applying for.

It's important to ask your agency the who, what and why. It's essential to be versatile, research what you're doing and reflect the client. You need to prepare in other ways, too. Plan your route; pack water (you may be waiting around for some time), a hairbrush and a hairband; and – trust me – take an umbrella. If you turn up looking like a drowned rat, your beauty regime was for nothing. Also, make sure you keep your portfolio/tablet clean and in good order. It's key to know who was involved in your previous shoots. You'll definitely be asked.

Lesson number four: fix up, look sharp

Your face, hair and nails need to be *squeaky* clean. It sounds so stupidly obvious, but if you walk into a room with greasy hair, you're telling the client two things. Firstly, you can't be bothered to wash. Secondly, you're clearly not a busy model and haven't worked in a few weeks. In the modelling world, your skin is so important. You need to lock down your skincare routine and follow it *religiously*. Here is a simple skincare routine that you can follow:

1. Take off all your make-up with a pH balanced cleanser, ensuring that there is no residue left. Wipe against gravity to prevent ageing. If your skin is oily or prone to spots, gel or foaming cleansers are probably better for you. They're designed for deep cleansing and are perfect for removing excess oil and unclogging pores. For those with dry skin, cream cleansers are ideal, because they remove the nasty stuff without stripping back your natural oils.

2. Toner is massively overlooked, yet massively important. Toners help close the pores that open up when cleansing, so nothing nasty can get in.

3. Moisturiser can double as a primer in the morning before you put on make-up. Oil-free moisturisers are great for people who struggle with spots. Try to avoid applying any moisturiser to your eyelids; it can make them look oily.

4. Experiment. There are a million different products out there. No two people's skins are the same, so you need to experiment to see what works for you and what doesn't. I've had products burn me or break me out, and some that haven't left my handbag since I bought them. For on-the-go skincare, hydrating sprays are incredible as they will brighten your skin before a casting.

Guess what we at Gingersnap end up repeating the most to people who come to see us? "Too much make-up." Model make-up isn't what they apply on Instagram or YouTube. It's all about emphasising and highlighting your features, not hiding anything. Here are some casting guidelines. Less really is more.

- Ditch the thick foundation. Save that bad boy for birthdays and Christmas. You don't want clients to think you're hiding anything. Let me introduce you to your new best friend: BB cream. It will even everything out without looking cakey. Alternatively, you can mix your regular foundation with some face cream to lighten things up.
- It's advisable to find a day cream or a BB cream with SPF (a light coverage foundation moisturiser.) You're always in the sun, and you need to protect your skin against sun damage.
- Use a small amount of concealer under your eyes and on any spots. With all face products, finding your perfect colour is vital. Make-up guru Bobbi Brown shares my philosophy on skin: it should look like skin. If you're unsure, pay your local department store a visit. The likes of John Lewis, Harvey Nichols, Selfridges and

House of Fraser will have a great selection of branded make-up counters.

- Cream blush on the apples of your cheeks looks natural and gives you a little glow. Apply cream bronzer to all the points of your face that would naturally be tanned by the sun (cheeks, forehead etc.).
- Light mascara. No spider legs here! Avoid false lashes at all costs.
- Tinted lip balm gives your face some life. Your cream blush can double as this when you're in a pinch.
- Use clear mascara to keep those pesky brows in place.
- Eye drops! They have two purposes: they brighten your eyes, and you can add them to an old, crusty mascara for some emergency rejuvenation.
- Clients want to see you as a blank canvas, not one that's already painted.

Hey! You're starting to resemble a real model. You're getting good at this!

Test Shoots

Test shoots – also known as time for print (TFP) – are the model's equivalent of an athlete going to the gym. It's practice – portfolio-building experimentation. Whether you're a brand-spanking-new model, or an old-timer who's got a new haircut or some new tattoos, testing is a great opportunity. Your portfolio (also referred to as your 'book') needs to reflect how you really look, so must be kept up to date. Not only that, clients want to see experience when booking a model. They want to see a varied range of pictures, facial expressions and poses. The only way to achieve this is by testing, testing, testing.

A test is exactly what it says on the tin. An experiment. An attempt. Practice for the real deal: paid jobs. Now, I know what you're thinking. Money rarely changes hands when testing (apart from on the occasions when your travel might be covered). So why on earth do it? As a new model, it's hard to know how valuable a test is. Believe

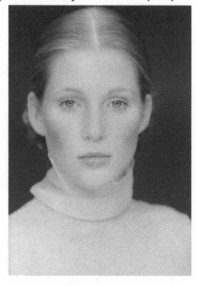

Picture by Nick Otley,
Clare's Sunday test shoot

me, they're worthwhile. Essentially, testing means taking your time to understand what kind of model you are, what you like doing and who you like working with. Tests will build your portfolio and your confidence in equal measure, preparing you for the working world. A test is essentially a job. It's constructive to frame it in this way because it will get you used to shoot etiquette and who's who on a shoot. It might be that on a test you form relationships with photographers or make-up artists who could end up getting you paid work. It's certainly not unheard of. Treat your tests as if they are jobs. Be prompt, professional and polite if you want to get the most out of them.

Once I agreed to test on a Sunday. I don't know what possessed me to go out the night before, but I had a bitter hangover that morning. My boyfriend drove me to London from our flat in Bristol, and I felt disgusting. But I can honestly say I made more money from that test shoot than I did from any other job. The pictures came out incredibly. My portfolio was so strong after that, and I got booked and booked and booked from it. I'm not advising that you go out and get plastered the night before a test shoot. But, honestly, it's worth doing every test that's offered to you because remember: just because they don't pay, it doesn't mean they won't pay off.

Your agency should send you a call sheet with all the information you need for a test, so you know where you need to be and when. But here are some key questions to ask:

- Who is the photographer? Have a major stalk of their portfolio to see if you like their work. If you don't like the photographer, you most likely won't like the outcome of the shoot, so avoid that test! Make sure they are creating the sort of imagery you want and – crucially – that will get you work.
- Is there a make-up artist? If there is, have a look at

their Instagram or ask your agency for a link to their portfolio. If there isn't a make-up artist, how should you do your own hair and make-up?

- Is there a stylist? There is? Good. Stalk, stalk, stalk. If there isn't, don't worry, but you'll need to see the mood board for style guidance. A mood board is a compilation of images which project the shoot's concept. The photographer should have given your agent a mood board to show you. If they haven't, ask for one! Pack as many clothes as you can – you'll most likely be shooting lots of different looks – but make sure that whatever you choose works with the style of the shoot. Your wardrobe will build up at the same time as your career. In the beginning, have some basic items like white shirts and jeans. Borrow, beg and steal from friends, and look out in charity shops for a few fabulous one-off pieces.
- Are there other models involved? This is always a great opportunity to trade tips, gossip and advice.
- Check the call sheet for location and time details. Plan your route and don't be late!

The team working on the test shoot will have been fully vetted by your agency, but if you're not represented yet, don't panic. It's really easy to organise your own test shoots. When doing so, the number one rule is: don't forget to be safe. It's advisable to research photographers and to always meet in public places. Instagram is a hotbed of young, eager and student photographers who want to test models, so you'll have plenty of choice In fact, a stunning test shoot that kick-starts your career may be only a DM away.

You've done all the hard work; now here are my top tips for

not being a deer in the headlights as soon as a camera is pointed at you. We've all been there!

Being in front of the camera

Some models know how to move in front of the camera. It's like acting, or mimicking accents: some people can just do it with no practice. They snap their fingers, and they can turn it on and off when they want to. But most of us are not that fortunate, and need to work at it!

I learned a lot from other models. Don't be scared to join the photographic team, who usually cluster around the monitor behind the photographer. From there you can hear the photographer's instructions and watch how the model interprets them, and you'll be able to see the slight variations in each shot as the model moves with every click of the shutter. It's also useful to collect magazines or catalogues and copy the poses the models make. See how they feel and how they look. The free magazines you get in high-street shops that advertise new collections are great for this. You can even order them online.

Never be afraid to ask questions on shoots. A shoot should be a team effort. The best photographers are those who put down the camera and physically show you what they want, but there

Picture by Nick Otley, Clare's Sunday test shoot

are others who won't say a word to you (I call these photographers 'click-click-click photographers'), and that's when you're on your own. But fear not – you can do it on your own.

On a *Vogue* shoot in Sydney, completely by chance, I learned a trick that changed my career. In previous shots we had used sheets of glass, and when they were all moved off the set, behind the photographer, the lights hit the glass at just the right angle. Bingo! I had a mirror and could see exactly what my body was doing in front of the camera, and guess what? Your pose looks different to how it feels. My movements were slightly exaggerated. The shoot went amazingly and completely transformed the direction of my career. From then on, the mirror was my best friend. I'd never looked in the mirror so much in my life. I knew what every angle of my body and face looked like. I practised for hours, so that when I got on set, all I had to do was pretend that the photographer was a mirror. From then on, I knew exactly what I was doing.

Bunch of bananas

Models are commodities. Being a commodity is a strange concept, because your thoughts and feelings about your image as a model are very different to those about yourself as a person. You should see your image as something external which almost belongs to the clients and customers to whom you are selling it. The bare-chested model opening his mouth and throwing down Diet Coke in the hot summer sun while being watched by a gaggle of women is an iconic piece of intellectual property worth millions. When you buy a Diet Coke, you are getting more than the Coke; you are also buying into a significant piece of popular culture. Models should commoditise themselves. It's hard to say 'commoditise' – and even more difficult to do it in practice!

Everyone around models has an opinion…and they are

entitled to it, because they are paying for you as a commodity to sell products. Allow it! It does take a while to get used to, though. As a young model, I worked with a photographer (let's call him Jim) for the teen magazine *Looks*. The photo involved me applying cream to my face. In no time at all, Jim shouted from behind the camera, "Your hands are like huge bunches of bananas, aren't they?" This comment made me more aware of my hands for the rest of my modelling career. At the time I was destroyed, but I soon learned that I shouldn't – no, *couldn't* – allow myself to be so sensitive about what clients said, because it was business. What I did do, though, was take Jim's comment and work on making my hands look as delicate as possible in pictures. The angle of models' hands should be carefully considered, with spaced out slightly bent fingers rather than straight clumped together digits. I even got booked for hand-modelling jobs! Take those lemons and turn them into lemonade, because it's the only way you can learn and grow as a model.

I must confess that, further into my career, my opinion sometimes got the better of me. I have very long legs, so I got booked a lot for hosiery campaigns. One particular time, I went to a huge casting. The client took my book and looked my legs up and down. I was wearing a very short skirt and, of course, had shaved and creamed my legs. The client remarked bluntly, "Well, you have quite a few moles on your legs, don't you?" I was taken aback, and instantly snapped, "Yes, I am human, you know!" Unsurprisingly, I didn't get that job! I should have smiled gracefully, but my comment just wouldn't stay inside my head. I should have been professional enough to bite my tongue, swallow my thoughts and concentrate on the money, honey!

Relax, listen, perform

You hold tension in your lips, arms, hands and shoulders. When in front of the camera, a model should be aware of all these areas. My shoulders would always rise, so I would roll them so that they would drop. Timid models have their own strategy for relaxing, whilst others don't get nervous at all. I find that chatting to the photographic team in the morning is great because you quickly get to know them. A nice cup of tea helps, too. Throughout the shoot, stretch your lips and shake your hands when you feel a little tense. You'll look crazy, but believe me, it works. A tried-and-tested warm-up trick utilised by actors is to speak the vowels out loud: "A, E, I, O, U."

One absolute non-negotiable is listening to the photographer's instructions. Being told what's required is a biggie. They might want more energy in the images, constant interaction with the camera, or for you to work in front of the camera like there's no one else watching. You can easily get stopped in your tracks in the middle of a picture and be asked to concentrate on a move or a vibe. I used to interpret the vibe by imagining myself in that particular situation. Drama buffs out there: get creative and think yourself into that role! I once did a shoot with a really cool photographer who wanted me to look like I was angry and shouting all day, so he played loud, heavy music to maintain a high energy. I got the gist straight away and we had lots of fun experimenting with different angry facial expressions and body poses. All that day I thought of people or situations I really hated and imagined I was yelling at them! Believe in yourself as a performer in front of the camera.

Be bold: get creative

Modelling is about navigating stereotypes whilst embracing your authentic self. It's about thinking creatively and coming up with movements and poses that will look great on film. Don't just jump to the most obvious move which any old model can do. You should fit within the brief, whilst allowing your own special sparkle to shine through.

As an older model I worked with a relatively young wedding photographer who'd been booked for a shoot for a sheepskin clothing catalogue. He was only used to shooting brides, so directed me into the bride-type poses which had worked for him before. I tried my best to navigate him away from pretty bridal poses towards more creative poses which sold the clothes rather than the model. There is a huge difference between the two! I was being paid to sell the clothes, not myself.

Face and body must come together as one to create the best imagery possible. Sometimes it can feel like patting your head and rubbing your tummy in one continuous movement for the whole day. It helps to feel what you're doing with your body so that it shows on your face. Concentrating on your body whilst keeping your face in check takes some practice. I learned this hard lesson when I shot a hosiery campaign. I turned up and the client showed me pictures of another red-headed model doing Irish dancing. She was dressed in red and was clearly an Irish dancer. That was a sink-or-swim moment! After an hour-long hair and make-up session, I put on the floaty red dress and off I danced. I'm not going to lie: that was a hard gig. I am not a dancer, trained or otherwise, so I was completely out of my comfort zone. I had to do the Irish jig whilst looking serenely happy. I thought my way into a *Lord of the Dance* vibe; lined up body, mind and spirit; and pulled it off – just!

At the beginning of this book I talked about being the awkward ginger kid at school. The very thought of me as an actual, real-life fashion model whom people paid thousands of pounds to take my photograph seemed insane. I remember when I first joined Models 1 aged fifteen, all my classmates found out and I heard the class joker say, "If I ordered a model and Clare Wilson turned up, I'd think it was a joke!" Well, I can tell you that years later when I was shooting for countless magazine covers, I used to think about that boy walking past a news-stand and seeing my face. But mostly, I used to think about the most wonderful, beautiful things so that my face was as serene and relaxed as possible. Cover shoots are all about the eyes – making them sparkle like marbles – so you should be thinking lovely thoughts. The skinny ginger kid came good – what do you think of me now?! And do you want to know the difference between the awkward girl with the bowl cut and the girl in *Vogue*, *Elle*, *Marie Claire*, and *She* magazine? In a nutshell, self-belief.

The Book

Your book (or portfolio), contains the best examples of your work. Ideally, you should carry your book with you to all castings, jobs and tests. You can have a physical book or a digital one. Plenty of models carry their books on a tablet – there are loads of portfolio apps. These are certainly easier to carry around on the Tube than a big, heavy file, and definitely better than a casting team bashing heads trying to see your pictures on a smartphone. Whichever format you choose, it must *always* be clean and presentable. I've cringed when models handed over bent, scruffy or dirty books (sometimes all three) to clients. First impressions count, and are sometimes all you have at a fast-paced casting. Your book is essentially your CV, and the client literally a potential employer. You need to convey that you are more than capable of becoming the face of a brand, and this starts with a squeaky-clean, killer book. Taking your book to a shoot should become a habit; it's commonplace for a team to refer to your book for make-up, hair or poses for their shoot. When the client needs to check out your book on a shoot, you quickly get it out. Like a pro.

How to put a book together

Putting your own book together is hard. Your personal feelings about a certain picture may contrast with what industry professionals want to see. Therefore, the best people to compile your book are your agents. They, more than anyone, know what needs to be in your portfolio, so listen to their advice. The next best person is a seasoned photographer, as they will know their way around a portfolio. You should see your book from a client's point of view: it needs to display a good cross section of your best work. One bad or weak picture will put the client off. Just because you've done a new test, it doesn't mean it should feature in your book. Only your strongest and most beautiful pictures here, please!

The regular format of a physical portfolio book is roughly twenty double-page spreads of gorgeous pictures that are ten by twelve inches. The book, or portfolio app needs to tell a story from start to finish, with your strongest headshot on page one, and a story that flows from there. Keep the different genres together if you can. An example book might contain:

- Headshot.
- Two killer full-length prints.
- Magazine tear sheets.
- One killer beauty shoot.
- Bridal shots.
- Action shots.
- Sports shots.

It's a good idea to set out all your pictures on the floor, then pair them up. Shots from the same shoots should be together. Heads in paired images should be facing inward, towards each other. Make sure the colours are complementary – no clashes! Black-and-white shots should always be together. Tear sheets and strong evidence of past work should feature heavily. Use nice advertorials, beautiful advertising shots, and only the most striking and current tests. Nothing in your book should be older than about two years.

Know who you worked with on each shoot that features

in your book – you will be asked. As you get more experienced, the names mount up, so keep them in a safe place so you can refer to them. Clients want to know: which photographer? Who did the make-up? Where was this shot? They'll be impressed if you know most of the people involved.

Portfolio apps

Models 1 card.
Picture by Thomas Krygier

There are a few portfolio apps available for various devices. Most models today carry around an iPad or other tablet to present their portfolio to clients at castings. Make sure the app is kept up to date with your agency book, and that it's similar to your page on the agency website. These apps are a great idea for a number of reasons:

- Good portfolio apps allow the creation of a number of books, so you can switch easily between books according to the client you are seeing (underwear, commercial, fashion…).
- A tablet is lighter than a paper portfolio and slips inside your bag for those long casting days.
- When you're hanging around at shoots and castings, the tablet doubles up as a source of entertainment.
- Images look *great* with light behind them; it kind of brings them to life.

Cards

Model cards are also known as:

- Z cards.
- Comp cards.
- Comps.
- Just plain cards!

These are essentially your business cards, which should be taken to every casting and given to clients as a 'calling card' to remember you by, or to write notes on during your meeting. Model cards are mostly A5 in size. Some clients may grab three or four cards. This means they are keen. As a model, it's your responsibility to always have plenty of cards on you.

Your agency should organise your cards for you. Some print model cards in bulk to distribute and to keep at their office. The model is charged the printing cost on their account with the agency, which means that the money is usually taken

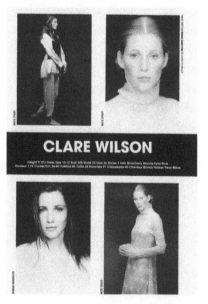

Pictures by Nick Otley and Sarah Maingot,
back of my card

out of future earnings rather than as cold, hard cash out of your pocket.

At Gingersnap, we try to be conscious of the environment: our models' cards can be found on their online portfolios, to be printed when needed or emailed as PDFs. A handful of cards should be kept in the sleeve at the front or back of your portfolio so that clients can help themselves. If you only have a digital book, keep a PDF of your card, including contact details and measurements, handy so that it can be easily shared with the client.

Whatever format you choose for your card, they should all contain the same information:

- Model's name.
- One main headshot.
- The four strongest portfolio images – at least one showing the body, and one three-quarter length.
- Model's accurate measurements (including height, bust, waist, hips, and clothes and shoe sizes), and eye and hair colours.
- Contact details for the agent (with their branding) or the model.
- Model's social media handles (optional).

Agencies

Scams

Admittedly, this is a dark way to begin this chapter. However, the modelling industry can look confusing from the outside, and to fully understand this wonderful world, you need to investigate its nasty bits. But don't worry – let me show you what I learned in the trenches, so that you don't have to experience the less savoury aspects of modelling.

So, why does modelling have a bad name? Without sounding too much like an A level sociology student, it's all about capitalism, really. The fashion industry (mostly) employs models who are size eight, five foot ten, super healthy, and young. The role of these aspirational models is to make you – yes, you! – feel that you would look better if you bought the product they're advertising; basically, to make you part with your hard-earned cash.

We all post pictures on Instagram looking fitter, skinnier, bustier, taller, happier, sexier and healthier than we are (ie, generally, massively altered), so we are all guilty of presenting the 'ideal' version of ourselves to the outside world. And why not? At the other end of the spectrum, the glamour industry generates bad press alongside its dark, seedy, exploitative cousin that it just can't seem to shake: porn. In truth, when your young son or daughter suddenly pipes up, "Mum, I want to be a model", you can definitely be excused if your heart sinks.

But fear not – I'm here for you. There are plenty of ways to stay safe out there. Here are some tips on spotting a fake agency:

- There is a (usually big) fee for the initial interview/casting, which they sell to you as a 'deposit'. Don't pay it. If there is a joining fee, don't pay. If there is a fee for portfolio shoots, don't pay. Just don't pay. Real agencies take commission out of your fee from a job, and pay you the rest.

- A response that comes *way* too quickly following your online application. Real agencies are busy and may take a few days or even weeks to get back to you. The real deal is worth the wait.

- They advertise for new models through click ads or social media. Real agencies have no marketing budgets; they are business-to-business (B2B) companies. The good ones don't have to pay to advertise because their clients (Asda, Panasonic, Dyson…) are the advertisers.

- Real agencies should have a list of clients on their website. These guys pay for models and come in many forms, from local small businesses to global corporations. Fake agencies' only clients are the models they scam.

- A fake agency will have no other named models listed on their website. It should be very easy to identify the models who are already with an established agency: their faces will be on the website!

- The office staff of a fake agency is made up of people who organise portfolio shoots that you pay for. In a real agency these people are bookers who will work on getting *you* paid for shoots.

- If they are calling you on weekends, that's usually not a great sign. Legit agencies' operational hours are Monday to Friday.

- Real agencies have a contract stating all their business practices, and/or a handbook that tells you everything you need to know. Fake agencies will not.

These so-called 'agencies' are essentially glorified photographic companies that provide a set of 'industry-worthy' images in exchange for an extortionate amount of cash. They call themselves agencies or 'model advice companies' but, in reality, they take pictures that are supposed to give you a better chance of catching the attention of proper agencies like Gingersnap. They are exploiting individuals who want to break into the industry but don't know how, and they have scammed a lot of people out of a lot of money. The final bitter truth is that real agencies don't want the type of pictures these scammers provide. All we want initially is regular, make-up-free snaps which can be taken on any mobile device.

Let me save you a *lot* of money:

- Find someone to help; literally anyone who can hold a camera or a phone. If you're paying them £500 an hour, you've taken a wrong turn somewhere. If it's your mum or your best mate in the living room, you're on to a winner.
- Go natural! Take off all your make-up (including fake lashes).
- Find a plain-coloured painted wall with nice, soft, filtered lighting. Stand in front of said wall.
- Relax. I always tell people to pretend the camera doesn't exist; act like you are just waiting for a bus.
- Try a variety of natural poses. Up close, full length, mid length (waist upwards), smiling, serious and relaxed.
- Stretch your lips or blow with them to release tension and then relax them. The way they are just after

relaxing them is the lack of stiffness you're going for. Pouting is fine, but keep it natural. Shake your hands every so often so that they relax too.

• Disable the flash and snap. No filters, no gimmicks, just you.

You now have a perfectly acceptable set of pictures to send to proper agencies, and I've just saved you thousands of pounds. You're welcome. But don't thank me just yet. We still have some research to do before we start applying to agencies…

Finding the right agency for you

When you are just starting out, finding the right agency can be a tricky business. Do you go for agencies that are affiliated with the British Fashion Council (BFC)? How do you know if an agency is the best one for you? How do you even know if they are reputable and will look after you and your career? Do not fear – I am here to help!

The British Fashion Model Agents Association (BFMA; formerly the Association of Model Agents) was established in 1974 to protect and manage models' careers. It is officially affiliated with the BFC. Membership requires signing up to and abiding by a set of criteria that protects the industry. Members can display the BFMA logo. Currently there are eighteen members – mainly fashion-based agencies.[1] As the BFMA is aimed at mostly high-end fashion model agencies, thousands of reputable commercial and fashion-based agencies (such as Gingersnap) choose instead to work in compliance with the Employment Agencies Act 1973 and associated Conduct of Employment Agencies and Employment Businesses Regulations 2003. The Act sets out employment business legislation wherein model agencies are required to

---

1   More information can be found at https://bfma.fashion/

abide by specified minimum standards of conduct, and the BFMA criteria are effectively the same as those in the Act.[2] So don't worry – just because an agency is not with the BFMA, it doesn't mean that they are not worth considering. It just means that, as a potential model, you should do your initial due diligence checks, and this is how.

Finding a reputable agency requires time and patience. Model agencies frequently change their names, and new agencies spring up on a weekly basis. The best advice I can give when looking for a suitable, reputable agency is to do your research:

- Look at the agency's website and the kind of models they represent. Realistically, does your look fit in with the looks and criteria of the models on the site?
- Does the agency have a registered office?
- How long has the agency been trading?
- Look on Companies House[3] at the agency's financial credentials.
- Does the agency have an initial application form, and ask for your ID? This is a government requirement.
- Are all the bookers Disclosure and Barring Service (DBS) checked?
- Carefully read the agency's terms of business and model agency agreements. Many agency agreements are similar, but red flags to look for are things like the agency fee they charge, and the amount of time it takes for a model to be paid. A reputable agency should have all their terms approved by legal professionals.

2   More information can be found at http://www.gov.uk/employment-agencies-and-businesses
3   https://www.gov.uk/government/organisations/companies-house

- Talk to the agency and ask what kind of jobs they are working on.
- Stalk their models' social media profiles. Most professional models mention their agency in their bios.
- Ask other models for their opinions on agencies.

Do some stalking

No, nothing sinister! Think of it as doing some background checks. The best-case scenario would be to meet a model who is represented by the agency and ask them for honest feedback on it. Also ask questions like: What's their relationship with the agency like? Are they working regularly? What's their client base like? Check if the agency is a registered company on Companies House, and look them up online. Read the 'about us' page on their website and do some serious digging on their social media platforms.

Here are some questions you may want to ask an agency themselves before you sign with them. Don't be afraid to call them if the information isn't online.

- Who are your clients?
- What was the last job you booked for a model?
- Who do you represent?
- Where is your office?
- Please can I see your model contract?
- Please can I see your client terms of business?
- What are your payment terms?
- What percentage do you take from models?
- How can I build my portfolio and is there a charge?

Et voilà! You're well on the way to becoming a represented model, and it hasn't cost you a dime.

Agency talk

It's Monday morning. What's on the Gingersnap to-do list? Office: unlocked. Kettle: on. Laptop: open… Oh, hey, I didn't see you there. Welcome to the agency; let me show you around.

What is an agency?

An agency can be a lot of things. It can be one person or a whole team, local or international. An agency is an office where bookers work to get their models castings, tests and jobs. Established agencies are fountains of knowledge, contacts and clients that should kick-start your career in the industry. By their very existence, agencies have a vested interest in creating a successful career for you. You make money; they make money. An agency makes a commission from your modelling jobs – anything from 20–50% of your fee depending on the kind of job and the location. A word of caution: make sure you check how much commission your agency is taking! Some European agencies have to take a much higher percentage (like 50–60%) to pay government taxes.

It's not you; it's me!

Just like models, no two agencies are the same, so it's really important to do your research and get recommendations from other, established models. It's important to join an agency you like the look of and meet your bookers. No agency will suit all models. You need to choose the best ones for you.

Bookers are your professional best mates. You might not know it, but they are talking about you all day long – how good you look, how good you *could* look, which shots are your best and how lovely your phone voice is. Your bookers decide your schedule, sell you to clients and negotiate your fees. Basically, they decide how much money you earn, so communication is the key to a fantastic relationship. Be available, be professional, be open and honest. The golden rules of making your booker your best friend:

- Be super, super hot on your emails and phone. I can't stress this enough. Your bookers need to know your availability ASAP; sometimes at very late notice. The models who are the best at getting back to their bookers get booked the most. Simple.

- If you know you won't be available for a period of time (no matter how long or short), ensure you 'book out' so you won't be booked on those days.

- If you don't want to do a job, let the booker know why so they can relay that to the client. If there are certain cultural or ethical limits to your potential modelling work – for example, religious beliefs regarding clothing, or ethical standards for the types of companies you want to work with – inform the agency in advance. As an agent, I can think of hundreds of reasons why a model wouldn't want to do a job – one that sticks out in my memory was a vegan model who was asked to hold a piece of meat in a picture. On the flip side, I can also think of hundreds more reasons why a model would still opt to do the job – coins, mostly, not to mention experience and great pictures. Your bookers work hard to secure bookings for you, so make sure your boundaries are crystal clear and understood by your team.

- Be flexible. Paid shoots are what you've worked so hard for! It's so important to grab every opportunity that you're offered. Turn down work a few times and agencies will stop putting you forward for jobs. On the other hand, it only takes a few last-minute bookings, or some great communication, to start building up a relationship with your agency. If you're known as a reliable model, bookers will trust you and put you forward for more work.

- When you have issues, don't panic. We are all human and sometimes life throws curveballs at us. The important thing is to communicate with your booker at the earliest opportunity, either to fix an issue or to find a replacement for a job. It's always better to call and have an honest conversation.

Trust me, great relationships with your bookers are so important. They are the key to your whole career. So bring your bookers doughnuts, wish them a happy birthday and compliment their killer outfits. A happy booker means a happy model, which, in turn, means a happy bank balance.

Small agencies vs large agencies: the pros and cons

Small Agencies	Large Agencies
More likely that the bookers will get to know you quickly.	More bookers; more opportunities.
Closer relationship with models.	Feels like you are a number.
More focused on models' careers.	Bigger jobs (and therefore more money).
Easier to talk through issues.	Represent better and bigger models.
Longer lifespan as a model.	Shorter career and fast burnout.

Are you receiving me?

OK, you have done your research, you know which agency you want to be with, you fit their criteria, and you want to make contact. What next? Many agencies have open castings in the mornings, or on certain days of the week. For others, you apply first with some digital snaps and wait to be called in for a meeting.

We've already talked through how to take killer pictures to send in to an agency, and these can be uploaded to an online application or sent directly to the agency in an introductory email. Here's the kind of thing you should say in your introductory email:

Dear Agency,[4]

Please find attached my digital snaps, taken today. My name is Amber and I'm twenty. My date of birth is xxxx and I live in Bristol, UK. I would love to come and see you at the agency at your earliest opportunity.

Many thanks,
Amber BC

Mobile number:

Not today, thank you!

You won't be every agency's cup of tea. The key is not to take rejection too personally. There are a thousand reasons why an agency might not take you on. It could be that you are too small or too commercial, or it could be that there is already a model on the agency's books who looks similar to you and is *killing* it. Whatever the reason, the agency should share it with you and give you some advice, including on other agencies you should consider. All this means is that the agency isn't right for you; it

---

4   Always find and use the name of the 'new faces' booker.

doesn't mean your career is over. Do. Not. Panic. Being rejected at any age is a hard pill to swallow. Believe me when I say that beauty is in the eye of the beholder and different agencies have varying markets. The biggest piece of advice I can offer is to learn to love 'no'. Make 'no' your best friend and turn it into a positive. That's easier to say than do, I know. You might not be right for one job, but you will be perfect for many others. Clients and agencies are focused solely on finding the right model for each job, with all the minute considerations that involves. Subsequently they are sometimes vocal about whether or not you fit that brief. Smile, nod and thank them for their time. Keep it professional and you will be remembered. Put your efforts into the next meeting or casting, and remain as upbeat as possible. There will be many times in your career when you will be faced with rejection. Models (in fact, anyone you see in the media, like actors, musicians, sportspeople, presenters and even verified social media personalities) have encountered rejection and the word 'no' countless times. What they have done, though, is navigate through each rejection to get to the magic word 'yes'. Keep going and you'll find your success, I promise.

If you *are* taken on, first of all, let me offer you a big yay! Congratulations – your foot is on the modelling ladder! Following the confirmation that they want to work with you, a reputable agency will email you a copy of their handbook. An agency handbook outlines what the agency expects from you, and gives details of accounts, bookers, email addresses and emergency contact numbers. It will explain how to conduct yourself and how the agency is managed. Different agencies have different operational infrastructures with which you will become familiar. Some have certain bookers for specific departments and others have all bookers booking all jobs.

An agency will have years of industry experience behind

them. As a young model, don't be afraid to ask them lots of questions about how things work. They will deal with a range of clients and should make your experience as smooth a ride as possible. They are there to guide you, so you should listen to their advice on all aspects of your career. They will call and tell you that you didn't get that job you really wanted, as well as share the great news when an option has turned into a confirmation.

Sometimes an agency will 'test' you before they take you on officially. This means that you will go to see clients and photographers, some of whom will shoot you, to see how you get on in front of the camera. The clients and photographers will feed back to the agency and share the pictures they took so that the agency can make a judgement on whether you will work well as a model.

The first five years of my modelling career were not particularly lucrative. I never seemed to get the jobs my peers were bagging and I didn't earn much money. I did test after test and slowly built up my book, gaining valuable experience all the time, and finally, aged about twenty, my career turned a corner and I began to be booked for lots of jobs. I was ready. But in the early days I didn't even think about giving up, and I certainly got used to 'no' (though obviously, I wasn't sure I loved it!). Modelling kept me from living a life in Taunton which I wasn't particularly fond of. I had no choice at all – it had to be a success – so I dug deep, worked hard and finally found my success.

In my early days at Models 1, I saw young models come and go, and get their hearts broken when things didn't work out. But, looking back, it's clear that the successful ones didn't give up. They joined an agency that was right for them, and then totally rocked it.

Contracts

The industry needs contracts to keep all agreements legal. There are many types of contract, which we'll run through now.

Agency contracts

All reputable agencies have some kind of contract for their models. Contracts are set out in different ways. Make sure you read all the small print, because it does differ from agency to agency. All agencies should keep records in accordance with the Employment Agencies Act 1973. This legislation requires employment agencies to abide by a specified minimum standard of conduct. The Employment Agency Standards (EAS) Inspectorate in the Department for Business, Energy and Industrial Strategy (BEIS) is responsible for enforcing the Act, and they regularly visit model agencies to ensure that laws are abided by. If you are in any doubt about an agency, ask them about this Act.

Here is a typical model/agency contract (warning: it's long!). It has been signed off with the BEIS Department, so compare your contract with this one.

GINGERSNAP
models

Artist Agreement
Creative Management Models
With offices at Unit 256 The Paintworks,
Bath Road, Bristol BS4 3AQ and
New Bond House, 124 New Bond Street,
London W1S 1DX
(referred to as the 'Agency')
AND
[Model Name]
(referred to as the 'Artist')

For and in consideration of the mutual promises contained within this agreement, the parties hereby agree as follows:

1. For the term of this agreement, the Artist hereby appoints and engages the Agency to act as the Artist's agent in the fields of modelling and advertising including work in TV commercials (referred to throughout as the 'Fields').

2. During the term of this agreement, the Agency shall advise and support the Artist in the selection or consideration of career opportunities, advertisers, and the selection or creation of vehicles for the Artist's talents. The Agency shall further provide guidance on matters relating to public relations, advertising, talents, including the formation of a book/portfolio, and shall represent the Artist to the Fields.

3. The Agency may procure on the Artist's behalf, and at the Artist's expense, such materials that are necessary to promote the career of the Artist, including (but not limited to) books/portfolios and cards.

4. The Artist agrees to seek the Agency's advice in regard to matters concerning the Artist's endeavours in the Fields. The Artist shall also disclose to the Agency any offer(s) of employment submitted directly to the Artist and agrees to refer all inquiries concerning the Artist's services direct to the Agency.

5. The Agency is hereby granted the right to use and distribute and allow or license others to make use of and distribute the Artist's name, portrait and pictures in connection with the advertising and/or publicity of the Artist in the Fields and in connection with the matters covered by this agreement.

6. The Agency may publicise that it is the Agent for the

Artist, and the Agency may render similar services for others, and engage in other related business or ventures.

7. The Artist agrees to provide the Agency with current photographs to include tear sheets/advertising, written or other related material for promotional use of the Agency and Artist.

8. The Artist authorises the Agency to sign any written documents relating to a booking/assignment, and any other engagements about which the Artist has been consulted and which the Artist has accepted.

9. This agreement also authorises the Agency to sign Artist releases on behalf of the Artist, and authorise reuse and residuals, whether originated by the Agency or not.

10. The Artist acknowledges that both agency fees and model fees will be invoiced by the Agency. Unless otherwise agreed at the time of booking, the model disbursement is included at [X]% and the agent's fee at [X]% of the invoice total.

11. The Agency will deduct from all assignments a fee of the maximum [X]% of all monies or other contributions received by the Artist, directly or indirectly, under all assignments entered into during the term of this agreement, specified in paragraph eleven (11) and subsequently paragraph twelve (12). In the event that the Artist is paid the full amount in cash from the client, the Artist acknowledges that this sum is inclusive of the Agency's commission and agrees to therefore reimburse the Agency directly.

12. The Artist hereby grants the Agency the right/ authority to collect all fees and monies earned or

accruing to the Artist from all sources governed by this agreement and to remit to the Artist the net fee after deducting the aforesaid commission. This limited right of authority includes the right of the Agency to deposit the proceeds in a general business account prior to remitting the balance to the Artist. The Artist also agrees to instruct clients during bookings/ assignments or on the release the Artist signs at the time of production to send all fees and monies due to the Artist directly to the Agency.

13. The Agency usually invoices clients one week (7 days) following completion of a job. This allows for accurate expense costs to be charged alongside the invoice. The Artist will therefore be paid once the invoice has been settled. The Artist acknowledges that this process takes on average 3 months from the day of the job. In general, payments are dealt with every 14 days. The Artist will be paid 10 working days after the payment has been received IN FULL from the client. In the event of payment by cheque, an extra 5 working days after the 10 days will be required to enable the cheque to clear.

14. In the event that Artists wish the Agency to withhold their monies for more than 30 days, a statement will be emailed to the Artist every 30 days.

15. As all fees paid to the Artist by the Agency are gross, it is understood and agreed that the Artist is self-employed and is therefore solely responsible for the payment of any taxes and National Insurance contributions in line with Inland Revenue rules.

16. It is the Artist's duty to register with HM Customs and Excise for Value Added Tax if their annual turnover

exceeds the minimum current annual turnover registration threshold. In the event of registration, the Artist shall supply the VAT number and VAT shall be added to all invoices which are issued on the Artist's behalf.

17. It is further understood and agreed that the Agency operates as an employment business.

18. The term of this agreement shall be made for the period that the Artist is presented by the Agency, commencing on this date. The Artist may terminate this agreement giving one week's (7 days') written notice, delivered by recorded mail to the agency Headquarters or via email. If the termination notice is received after a booking/assignment has been arranged, the Artist agrees to honour that booking/ assignment or else reimburse the Agency for any and all costs incurred or revenue forfeited (including such revenue which may be owing to a client due to incurred expenses as a result of the Artist's cancellation). In addition, should, for whatever reason, the Artist and/ or Agency terminate this agreement, any fees owing to the Artist will be paid by the Agency immediately after payment is received from the client.

19. The Agency may terminate this agreement giving one week's (7 days') written notice, delivered by recorded mail to the Artist's address or email address held on record.

20. The Artist agrees to inform the Agency of any changes in their availability (e.g. holidays and other forms of employment), giving as much advance notice as possible. The Artist may also notify the Agency of particular clients for whom the Artist does not wish to

work. The Artist also acknowledges that once an offer has been accepted in respect of a booking/assignment, the Artist agrees to honour their obligations in accordance with this agreement.

21. Should the Artist fail to attend a booking/assignment, the Artist agrees to abide by such terms as may be renegotiated by the Agency and client.

22. In the absence of termination notice by either party, this agreement shall continue to be renewed from year to year on the anniversary date unless otherwise specified.

23. The Artist agrees to conduct themselves professionally at all times with dignity, and to do nothing on an engagement or otherwise that may tend to injure the reputation and goodwill of the Artist or the Agency, nor to partake in any act which impairs the Artist's capacity to fully comply with the terms of this agreement, or which impairs the Artist's qualities and abilities. The Artist further agrees to abide by the standard Terms of Reference outlined in *The Model* handbook with regard to behaviour on bookings/assignments. The Agency may, upon one week's (7 days') notice, terminate this agreement with the Artist for breach of this paragraph.

24. The Artist agrees that in the event any company other than the Agency offers gifts in the form of training or hospitality in connection with the modelling industry, the Artist will, before accepting any such gifts/hospitality, consult with and obtain the permission of the Agency.

25. The Artist confirms that once a client or photographer has been introduced by the Agency, any future

Artist work undertaken through this contact must be directed through the Agency during the term of this agreement. The Agency may, upon one week's (7 days') notice, terminate this agreement with the Artist for breach of this paragraph.

26. This contract sets forth the entire agreement between the parties. Should any provision(s) of this agreement be held to be void or not enforceable, such provisions shall be deemed omitted and this agreement with such provision omitted shall remain in force. No modification, alteration or amendment of any provisions contained within the agreement shall be valid or binding unless in writing by both parties. By entering into this agreement both parties agree that they have not been encouraged by, and are not relying on, any promises or representations not set forth in writing.

27. The Artist agrees that any test or experimental photography organised by the Agency will be subject to an exclusivity period of six months, where the images are not permitted to appear on any other model agency website, unless written permission is given by the Agency (Gingersnap Models).

28. The Artist acknowledges that, whilst potential clients are believed to be reputable and creditworthy, the Agency does not guarantee, and is not responsible for, the payment of fees and expenses in relation to such engagements. The Artist also agrees that the Agency shall not be liable should any engagement prove unsatisfactory in any respect.

29. The Artist agrees that Gingersnap is their 'Agency' and to namecheck them on any work involving Gingersnap

on their model profiles on social media, and will direct inquiries from clients back to the Agency.

30. This agreement shall be binding upon both parties.

NDAs

An NDA is a non-disclosure agreement. You might have to sign an NDA if you are doing a shoot whose products or concepts are confidential. The contract ensures the shoot team's secrecy regarding the nature of the shoot. As an agent, I often sign NDAs. It is normal practice when new and exciting products are launched into the marketplace.

Moving on

As elsewhere in life, the relationship between a model and an agent can break down. This can be heartbreaking (for both sides), but it's a normal part of the industry. Models sometimes move on, and that phone call or email telling your booker that you are leaving won't be their first or last of that nature. Joining a new agency can provide a model with a fresh lease of life – particularly if things have grown stale, or there's been a falling-out or disagreement.

It's advisable to go into your existing agency and talk things through with them face to face. However, if this is too painful for whatever reason, an email stating that you are moving on will ensure that everyone knows where they stand. This way there is no bad feeling and you can leave on good terms.

Dear [Agent Name],

I would like to give you my notice as representing me from today ([date]).

*Many thanks for the time I have had with you, and all
the best for the future.*

Love,
[Model Name]
xxxx

As an agent, I like to leave the door open for models to return.
I have lost count of the models who've emailed me and asked to
come back! Because we parted on good terms, the door is open,
and this is made clear to the model when they leave. I always feel
great when models come back to Gingersnap. It means that they
were happy here and they miss the Gingersnap team. It's like
baby ducks returning to their mama as grown-ups!

The key thing to remember is that your relationship with
your bookers is a two-way street. Treat your bookers well and
you will be looked after.

Shoots

Be prepared

So you've got the awesome agent and the killer book with model cards. I'd say that you're ready for the big time...now, where do you go from here? Well, if I can impart one thing to you, it's this: be prepared. Be prepared. *Be prepared!* In fact, in my opinion, you can't be prepared enough. Once you take your foot off the gas and sit back to relax, things can soon start to unravel. A few nights out; turning up to shoots still half-cut, tired, scruffy and unprepared for that bikini shoot...need I go on?! Success is not a final, defining moment; it's an animal which needs to be fed constantly. Come on, take my hand and welcome to the unofficial Clarey School of Successful Modelling, and let's feed this tiger!

First, let's talk sleep. I don't want to sound unnecessarily fussy, but you need your eight hours a night. The right amount of sleep means your eyes will be bright and your skin fresh, and you'll be ready for whatever the day throws at you. Make-up artists used to tell me all the time that make-up doesn't sit well on parched or tired skin. And they know.

This sounds obvious, but make sure you're clean from top to toe. When I'm giving models the details for a shoot, I always say, "Clean hair and face!" This way your team start the shoot with a clean palette.

Plan your route. Allow for commuters, and know where

you are going and how you are getting there. Of course, you can only plan for so many eventualities. Trains get cancelled and accidents happen every day. If you think there is going to be a delay, it's okay. Call your agency or client and explain what's happened. Try to remain calm! My worst 'late moment' has to be the time I was four hours late for a British Airways campaign shoot. My train was delayed and all I could do was sit there and wait. It was the longest four hours of my life, but I got there in the end and stayed later to make up for the time lost. Go, apologise profusely, and get on with the job in hand.

Things to take to a shoot in your modelling bag:

- Portfolio.
- Phone.
- Umbrella. (You don't want to turn up drenched if the Great British weather doesn't play ball!)
- Personal alarm (could be on a key ring or a phone app.)
- Money/bank card.
- Flesh-coloured underwear (including a strapless bra).
- Small bag with the essentials: lip balm, moisturising cream, hairbrush and razor.
- Anything specific your agency or the client has asked you to take for the shoot.

That's you! You're all set; let's get going!

Shoot day

You've been booked on the shoot, you have the details, you know what you're doing – now let me show you around the studio and introduce you to the team...

The client

This is the company or person who's paying for the shoot and needs the images for their brand. In short, the company you are working for. It should go without saying that these people deserve your utmost respect, but bear this in mind. As the saying goes, the client is always right. So, be nice, smile and be polite.

It could be one client or a bunch of them. They could be wearing cool casual clothes, or suits and office wear, looking very important behind their laptops. On an editorial/magazine shoot, the client is the fashion editor. On a larger advertising shoot, the client could be a freelance art director, the Producer, Director or the photographer. The photographer and team will liaise with the client to achieve the best images possible. The client might not always be present at the shoot, but there will always be someone representing them on site.

When you walk into the studio in the morning, you will be introduced to a whole sea of faces and names. Unfortunately, what is not often said is, "Here's Egle, she's the client. This is Muhammed, he's the photographer..." You will have to decipher who's who throughout the day. You can, of course, look at the call sheet and learn everyone's names, but the general rule of thumb is this: be super nice to everyone, because absolutely anyone could be the client. As the day progresses, it will become abundantly clear who is who.

The photographer

This is the person with the camera! They usually carry the whole shoot, by which I mean that they are the anchor of the shoot. It could take place at their studio or on location, but this pivotal person is the key member of the team. For smaller shoots, the photographer will have been commissioned by the client. On larger shoots, they work alongside the art director and client to create the images with the whole team. The photographer has been booked for their style of photography. They work on a freelance basis, so will have done a lot of prior work, had numerous meetings with the client, and worked as hard as you to be chosen for the shoot.

As a model you will work closely with the photographer. Your aim is to build a working rapport with them to allow the team to produce the best possible imagery for the client. There is definitely creativity involved in modelling – despite the ridiculous assertion that models are nothing more than dispensable coat hangers. The photographer may have some great ideas about how you should pose, or you could add your own ideas to make some beautiful pictures. Different personalities make for different images, so don't be afraid to ask the photographer questions and experiment with pushing some of their ideas. Some photographers provide lots of ideas; others say nothing at all. The best scenario for me as a model was when the photographer physically got in front the camera and demonstrated whilst explaining what was required. At these points there was no question at all about what they wanted. As a professional model you should interpret and execute what is required of you. This is, ultimately, what you are being paid for.

The make-up artist (MUA)

Make-up artists are responsible for making up models before and during the shoot. Once they have fully made up the models, they will be on hand with make-up brushes and powder puffs to take the shine off noses and correct anything else that needs attention. More shine, less sheen, lips brighter, eyeballs whiter… they are the shoot magicians who work their magic to make the models look their best.

Make-up artists are highly creative and talented people. It's a good idea to tell them at the beginning of the shoot if you are allergic to any make-up or any particular beauty products. All make-up artists have a different way of working, but they should ask you if you are allergic to anything in order to avoid a reaction which could jeopardise the day. Always start the day with a clean, fresh and moisturised face.

The make-up chair is usually a high director's chair or a bar stool with a backrest, in front of a large mirror with lights around it. It is high to allow the make-up artist to stand and work. Make-up artists work in close proximity to your face, so think about your breath – if you had a curry the night before, pick up some mints on the way to the shoot. The same applies to smokers – in fact, it's more polite to wait until the next natural break, or lunchtime, before having a cigarette. Smoking, eating or drinking whilst your make-up is being done isn't a great idea as your face needs to remain still. It might be better to wait until your hair is being done before you have a slurp of your cup of coffee. Most make-up artists carry straws for models so they don't mess up their lips. Real professionals carry environmentally friendly straws with them. Why not beat them to it by having a couple in your bag?

Make-up and hair can take approximately one hour each to complete, so get ready for at least two hours of pampering.

The hairstylist

The hair artist works at the smaller chair at the mirror, as they need you to be at a lower level to get to your hair. Again, if you are allergic to any hair products or hairbands that you know of, or sensitive to heat, you should let the hairdresser know so that they can plan their work accordingly.

The hairdresser will decide with the client how your hair should be arranged. It will be curled, straightened, finger-waved, combed, brushed, or just styled as is. They will work alongside the make-up artist to create the right look for the shoot.

As tempting as it is, avoid touching your hair throughout

the day, as the hairdresser has it covered. Your hair is their work for the day, so leave well alone.

The stylist

This is the person who buys and borrows all the clothing for the shoot. They will have spent quite a few days, or sometimes weeks, prepping clothes, shoes and looks for the shoot day. They have a few clothing rails, suitcases of clothes and a steam iron at hand.

The unsaid clothing rules:

- Don't comment negatively about the clothes. The stylist is working to a brief, so these are the clothes which are required. The designer has been designing and looking at their collection for many months, so please avoid any disparaging comments. Only compliments here!
- Once dressed, do not sit, eat or smoke while wearing the clothes. They have been washed and/or pressed, and any crease or mark *will* matter!
- If you have been asked to bring any clothing yourself, make sure it has been cleaned and pressed. Same with shoes: they should definitely be clean and polished. Invest in a suit bag and a carry-on suitcase so you're all good to go.
- As a model, you don't get to choose what you wear on a shoot. The stylist is there to put looks together – so sit back and enjoy being dressed, primped and preened.
- Between shots, change as quickly as possible, taking great care to avoid messing up your make-up and hair. In the '50s and '60s all models were expected to carry a 'changing scarf' with them; this was a thin silk scarf you used to preserve your hairstyle and make-up by putting it over your head, then taking off or putting on your clothes over the scarf. These days I wouldn't

say that you particularly need to carry a changing scarf around with you. Some stylists carry a scarf for this purpose – just so you know what's happening if the stylist comes at you with one!

- Wear clean underwear and take a spare pair. Always wear flesh-coloured or pale, minimal, unseamed underwear so it doesn't show through the clothes.
- Take a selection of underwear – strapless bras in white and flesh tones, and flesh-coloured pants. Believe me, they might seem like little touches, but you will impress the client and look professional.

The assistants

These are very important people. Everyone on the team of creatives could very well bring an assistant on set with them, especially the photographer, who needs help with lighting, their computer, their camera and the sets. There are many people who want to get into the industry, and the only way to get breaks and meet people is to assist. I know plenty of very established photographers who still assist their contemporaries. Make-up artists, hairdressers and stylists could all have assistants with them.

Why are assistants important people? Well, these guys are tomorrow's clients and photographers. Give them the respect they deserve. Not only are they being paid next to nothing for strapping your foot into that shoe, but they are potentially your prospective clients.

The film set team

The first time I was on a film set, I was blown away by the number of people involved, and the ways in which these sets differ massively from a regular stills photography set. These guys are hardcore!

The first thing to notice is that there is a definite hierarchy. In modelling, 'above the line' refers to the use of the imagery or footage. In the film industry it means something totally different; namely, the creative individuals at the top who have authority on set: the producer, the director, the client. 'Below the line' here refers to the shoot crew (like the runners and the boom operators), who are lower down the hierarchy.

Here is a list of the jobs on a film set, starting above and finishing below the line:

- **Executive producer:** Finances the film. Could be a business or a CEO.
- **Production manager (PM):** Responsible for the physical aspects of the production, like personnel, technology and budgets.
- **Director:** Responsible for bringing the story to life on screen.
- **Assistant director (including first and second AD):** Assists the production director and the manager. In charge of the day-to-day management of the cast and crew, including scheduling, sets and equipment.
- **Production assistant (PA):** Assists the first assistant director with the set.
- **Grips:** The lighting and rigging technicians who are responsible for all the lighting and camera equipment rigged over the cast and crew. There are several roles for grips:
    - **Key grip** is in charge of the grip department.
    - **Best boy grip** assists the key grip and oversees the rental of equipment on set.
    - **Dolly grip** operates the camera cranes and dollies (rigs holding the cameras).
- **Gaffer** is the head of the electrical department.

- **Best boy electric** assists the gaffer and is responsible for the daily running of the lighting, and hiring and scheduling of the crew.
- **Director of photography (DP):** Responsible for the translation of the script into visual images based on the director's requests.
- **Camera operator (CO):** Works closely with the director of photography to determine the composition of each shot.
- **First assistant cameraman (first AC or focus puller):** Knows and understands all the professional motion camera equipment used in the industry. Reads the script and recommends specific equipment.
- **Second assistant cameraman (second AC or clapper/loader):** Prepares the camera package along with the first assistant cameraman.
- **Loader:** Loads, unloads and labels all film canisters during filming, as well as preparing deliveries for the lab and delivering to production at the end of each shoot day.
- **Location scouts:** Work with producers and directors to choose the best location for the shoot in terms of aesthetics and feasibility (e.g. power sources, car parking facilities and location size).
- **Location manager:** Responsible for making all the practical arrangements for the location. Obtains fire, police and other governmental shoot permits and coordinates the logistics for the production to take place.

Money and Business

From the age of sixteen, I spent my summer holidays in London. I lived in an agency flat in Chelsea, and I'm sure the agency told my mum I'd be looked after. An agency flat is an apartment the agency owns or rents for new models. Rent for the flat was taken out of any model earnings. The truth was somewhat different. Although I wasn't *not* looked after, in reality I was just given a key to the door and told which bunk to sleep in, and to call the agency twice a day. My lunch was a cereal bar and a carton of Ribena, and supper consisted mainly of beans on toast or pasta. My mum gave me money at the beginning of the summer to live on, which I put aside and dipped into throughout the months so I had enough for food and travel. They were mainly happy summers, but I wasn't very successful as a model because I was learning. I didn't make a bean modelling back then. But that was okay. I was building up my portfolio and getting valuable industry and life experience; a bit like casing out the joint whilst I waited for success. If there was any chance of earning money from babysitting, I would take it.

One day, my friend Louise's boyfriend Steven[5] was at the flat. He was a really cool, fun twenty-year-old who scared the hell out of me – for a sixteen-year-old girl from the countryside, the gap between our ages felt cavernous! Steven was a very successful model with a different agency from us.

5   Name changed.

He was a fun Jack-the-Lad Londoner and seemed grown-up and worldly. That day in the early summer of 1989, we were hanging out outside the flat when Steven declared that he needed to get home but didn't have any money.

"Clare, have you got a tenner you could lend me?" he asked with a cheeky grin.

"No way!" I replied, thinking about how I had to eke out the money my mum had given me.

He wasn't going to give up that easily, though. "Look, I can pay you back tomorrow, I promise. I'll leave my Rolex with you and my leather belt," he said, looking down at the most valuable things he had on him.

Thinking that the offer was quite hilarious, and deciding that he would definitely come back for the watch and the belt, I agreed to the deal. I gave Steven a £10 note, and he handed me the heavy, hot leather belt from his jeans, along with the equally hot watch from his wrist.

The next day, as I was sitting on the steps outside the flat, an open-backed bus – the number 11 – flew by with Steven hanging out the back, waving at me. He hopped off and came running towards me waving a £10 note. "Told ya!" he laughed in his thick London accent.

A few weeks later during that long, hot summer, Steven piped up, "My agency is having a party tonight on a boat. Why don't you come?"

That evening, he came round and told us that he had a friend who wanted to go out but needed a babysitter. Another model, Sam,[6] and I replied in unison, "I'll do it!" So we went to this huge house to babysit whilst everyone else partied. When the parents came back at the end of the evening they paid us £20 which we split, then we left and that was that.

---

6   Name changed.

The next morning, back at the agency flat, we woke to absolute chaos. Steven's girlfriend Louise, who also lived there, was screaming and crying. Sam and I scrambled into her bedroom.

"There's been an accident. The boat the party was on has sunk and I haven't heard from Steven!" she sobbed.

Sam and I looked at each other in disbelief. Back then, of course, it was before the internet and twenty-four-hour news channels, and news took longer to filter through. So later that day we went to the *Evening Standard* newspaper stand and picked up a copy of the paper.

We pored over the story with our hands over our mouths, silent tears falling down our cheeks. It was true: there had been a terrible accident on the Thames. In the early hours of the 20 August, fifty-one people had been killed when the *Bowbelle*, a river dredger, ploughed into and immediately sank the *Marchioness*, a pleasure boat that was hosting a birthday party attended by more than 130 people. The party was for someone with close links to the modelling industry. As such, the *Marchioness* was packed with young fashion industry professionals – photographers, agents, models, make-up artists – and the average age of those who perished was a barely imaginable twenty-two. Some partygoers who were on the deck when the *Marchioness* was hit had been thrown in the water. Steven had been on the dance floor below deck and, incredibly, managed to get out. Unfortunately, the Thames' current was way too strong for him, and he died nonetheless. His body, along with others, was dragged far along the Thames and wasn't recovered for days. Poor Louise was in bits until finally the news came that his body had been found.

That summer I learned quite a lot; not only about the modelling life, but about life (and death) in general. The industry is filled with wild and wonderful people. Creative people are the craziest, and the goal is to negotiate yourself through their world and get the most out of your experience without ending up broke – or broken.

In terms of money, if you are successful, you are likely to earn a lot of it in a very short amount of time. But it's not about the amount of money; it's what you do with it. Many successful models I knew used to spend their money as soon as they earned it. In the late '80s and early '90s this meant personal Sony CD players, CDs, clothes and shoes. I used to look at them wide-eyed, thinking, If I had that much money, I would definitely save as much as I could. My philosophy has always been 'Spend a little, save a lot'. It is better to have a goal to save for. I wanted to buy a car and then a house – those were my goals! It wasn't until much later in my career, when I was working all over the world for German catalogues, that I earned the big bucks and eventually saved enough for a car and a few houses. Looking back, if I'd had the confidence then that I have now, I would have told the young models who were spending all their money as fast as they were earning it to save some. When you're young and suddenly earning very large sums, you never think it's going to end. But in all likelihood, it will end, and I imagine those models never earned that much money again. So, please, please, please save your money and set yourself up for the future.

Treat it like a business

Treat this industry like a business and it will pay you like a business. Treat it like a hobby and it will cost you like a hobby.

When you get the shoot details from the client or agency, note everything down, from the photographer's name to anything particular you need to take with you. For commercial modelling you'll be expected to take things to the shoot, so it's worth keeping a set of up-to-date clothes for any occasion so you can turn up prepared. Examples are:

- Smart jeans.
- Boots.
- A generic swimsuit.
- A warm coat (can be used to keep warm around the set, too!).
- Office clothes.
- Ironed white shirt.
- Black, nude and white underwear.

This is a serious career and should be treated as such. Castings are like interviews. Go alone and prepared. Do not take your dog, baby, granny, mum or cousin, because no matter how much the casting team will say it's cute and cuddly, *you will not get that job*! Take it from me: I've battled across London with a pushchair to countless castings, and not once did I get one of those jobs. You are much better on your own because you won't be stressed out. You will be relaxed, confident and able to concentrate on the job at hand: that important casting which gets you the gig.

Another key organisational skill: keep a diary! Whether electronic or an old-fashioned paper one, you should be getting everything down in that bad boy:

- The fee, and when it will be paid to you after your agency deduct their percentage.
- Usage of the images – is it worldwide, or will they be used locally, and for how long? This is your image, so you need to know what is being paid for.
- Are you doing stills, or moving-image work?
- The client's name – everyone loves being called by their name!
- When will the images be used? The client may not

know this initially, but in the months after the shoot, ask your agency so you can chase down some copies for your portfolio.

Remember: you have been paid for this shoot, so are not automatically entitled to use the images. The rights to the images belong to the photographer and the client, not you. You give up the rights to your image when you accept the fee. The client may let you have the images for portfolio use only. If the shoot is for a magazine, buy that magazine! These images are more useful than any others because they prove that you are a working professional model. Only use the best images, of course.

When you have downtime between shoots, use it wisely. Do not rely on your agency alone to fill your time. As a model you are a self-employed, which means you are ultimately in charge of yourself. Chase the pictures you know will be good from shoots you have done in the past. These images will fill up your portfolio and help to build your brand. Make some goals, organise your week, and stay focused!

Study

As we're on the subject of using quiet period's wisely, you have plenty of time to study as a model. At Gingersnap, some of the best models are students because they have time between lectures and are very happy to earn the money! There is no need to give up college or University to start a modelling career, as the two work in unison. If you are doing your A levels, model in school holidays and weekends. University students have more flexibility and very long holidays with short semesters. I went to the University of Winchester to do my degree in Film Studies after a year in London modelling and soon realised that work life was much tougher than being a student! I had spent a year working and living in London after my A levels, and modelling wasn't even covering my rent! I had to get a part-time job at a pub near my rented room just outside Parsons Green Tube station. That year was stressful and hard! It was no mistake that Winchester is only an hour's train ride to London either. I was constantly on the train between Winchester and London. Remember that there is life outside and after modelling. The day could come when you need a career change, and that diploma or degree in your back pocket will feather your path. If any agent tells you to give up education, I would be thinking twice about their true intentions. Education comes first and everything else will follow.

If education isn't your jam, there are plenty of other hobbies and side hustles you could be doing. I had a lot of respect for a model who spent six months earning a lot of money modelling, saving up as much money as possible, filling up a lorry of blankets and aid, and driving to various countries in need. A lady who took the huge model fees of the '90s to benefit people who really needed it – wonderful!

When you first start out as a model, the money doesn't come rolling in from day one, it's a long game. It's tricky to balance being available for potential jobs, keeping your head above water financially whilst still remaining fresh and looking the best you can. Unless you have parents to support you, a part-time job is a great option. Most modelling jobs are weekdays, which leaves your weekends free to pursue little bar or store jobs. You could have other side hustles, like social influencing gigs, singing, acting or selling artwork on Etsy, the list is endless! In fact, these 'side hustles' could very well define you as a model, you know, give you an edge! Something to talk about at those all important castings. Use it to your advantage rather than defining it as an extra income stream. So many people give up modelling in the early days because they think that they'll earn plenty of money and don't want to take other work to supplement income whilst they're starting out. Best case scenario, you get booked for a job, the job is invoiced the same week. Guaranteed that invoice will not be paid for maybe a month or more. Patience and hard work are the keys to success.

Another question I get asked is 'Can I have more than one agency?' The answer is 'Yes!' Work opportunities need to be maximised, and different clients have varying clients. Keep a tight diary, and communicate your availability to all agencies. My suggestion is to join a different agency in every main city. Your agency will have links with other agencies they like working with, so ask them for suggestions and they should be on hand to support you.

Tax

Tax can be a complicated affair, especially as models often work overseas. Different agencies and countries have different rates and commissions. As a self-employed model, it's up to you to keep up to date with any laws and rules. The most important thing to bear in mind is that you are responsible for your own taxes. There are plenty of websites from which you can get advice – the most important one being your local government website. One of the key UK sites is GOV.UK.[7]

At Gingersnap, models often ask us to explain how tax works, and whether we handle tax affairs too. So, let's run through some basics. As we're a UK company, that is the country we'll be talking about here.

Firstly, on every assignment booked through the agency, the models are not employed by us. They are generally either

---

7   See their 'Self Assessment tax returns' page, for example: https://www.gov.uk/self-assessment-tax-returns

a self-employed sole trader or, if they have set up their own limited company, an employee of that company. Therefore, each model needs to set aside some of the money earned from each job to pay tax to His Majesty's Revenue and Customs (HMRC). No tax is due on the first £12,571 as part of your personal allowance,[8] but thereafter 20% income tax is due up to around £52,270. After this amount, 45% tax is payable up to £150,000. If you get to that level, then congratulations – you can consider yourself one of the country's top models, as only a small percentage get to this point. If you earn above £80,000 you will also need to register for VAT. Something else to bear in mind: if modelling is a second career then you will probably use up your tax-free personal allowance in your first employment. You must also ensure that you are paying National Insurance, which entitles you to various state benefits. You pay Class 2 contributions if you make profits of £6,725 or more per year, and Class 4 contributions at 10.25% for profits you make of between £11,909and £50,276 per year. For higher earners there is an additional 2% of profit due. Please note that these figures are correct at time of writing and are reviewed regularly.

This could be the only time in your life when you have the capacity to earn vast sums of money in a short amount of time. As agents we deal with model fees ranging from £100 to £100,000. The fee is very much dependent on where the images will be displayed, for how long and in which countries. Believe me, it is in you and your agent's interest to get the largest possible fee for a job! Having been an agent for twenty years, negotiating fees is one of the best parts of my job. There is *always* some kind of budget – small, large or medium – for a commercial shoot, but there will be the odd time when a shoot happens with

8   The allowances change, so do check the government website: https://www.gov.uk/income-tax-rates

a fantastic team, and everyone is guaranteed amazing pictures for their books in return for their time only. When this is the case, speak to your agency. They will be best placed to make the call as to whether the unpaid shoot is worth your time (see also the 'Test Shoots' chapter).

Paid in full

Fees can be a hard one to get your head around. Many times, the fees are client led. Gingersnap gets emailed a brief with the model budget, which we work to. Sometimes clients shop around agencies to get the best price for models. In this case, each agency has an internal criterion based on where the images or footage are being used. Some things to consider when thinking about model fees:

- Where in the world will the images be shown? This could be locally, nationally or internationally.
- On which platforms will the images be used? Social media only? Press advertisements? Point of sale?[9] A huge billboard campaign?
- How many days will you be on the shoot? If it's a five-day shoot, for example, it will likely be paid as a day fee (basic studio fee), plus a usage fee as above.
- Are the images stills or moving? If moving, which TV channels will they appear on, and will they appear in cinemas? If so, internationally or nationally? If internationally, in which countries?
- What is the timeline for the images/footage? Six months? A year? Three years? Five years? In perpetuity?[10]

---

9   In shops where products are sold.
10   Forever.

The Usefee.tv website[11] is a very useful tool in terms of TV usage because it's a handy yardstick with which to calculate an appropriate use fee for TV commercials based on the established industry-endorsed method approved by the Personal Managers' Association and the British Fashion Model Agents Association.

The client must be transparent from the outset about where the images or footage will appear. It's best practice for the agency or model to inform the client on fees/costs etc. based on the usage. Clients will generally ask for quotes for a day fee, plus one-, three- and five-year options. A contract must always show exactly what is being used and where, so there is no doubt at all. The confirmation is legally the licence for the client to use the model's pictures or footage. The model and the agency should be in full agreement on the fee and usage (or potential usage) before the shoot happens so there is total transparency.

If you don't have an agency yet and are negotiating your own fees, be very careful and bear in mind the points in the list above. If you do the job and there is no paperwork or confirmation setting out the financials (alongside all other considerations), it will be very hard to go back afterwards to negotiate more money. Always, always, always have a paper trail, even if it's on email. That way both parties know where they stand even before the shoot happens. Never arrange to do a shoot for a product or a commercial client if you haven't negotiated a fee. There will be someone somewhere along the line making a lot of money from you. Remember, as a professional model your face and body are now a commodity, and you must treat them as such. If someone is making money from your image, you should be the first in line to collect your share of that money! If you are in any doubt, ask the question before the shoot happens. This is your business, and fees are the very reason you are doing the job.

---

11   http://www.usefee.tv/

So, which jobs pay more money?

Mode Magazine, Australia

Without question, the highest-paying jobs are the ones which have the greatest public reach. TV reaches approximately 70% of Europe's population daily, and the average person's weekly viewing time is three hours and thirty-nine minutes.[12] TV is the most powerful form of advertising, which means big bucks for sales, of which you are entitled to your slice.

The higher the profile of the campaign, the higher the fee. If you are featured in an advert shown during prime-time hours, you should get a usage fee each time the ad is aired. If you shoot a campaign for billboards across every city on the globe, your money should reflect that – think thousands. If your image appears in Times Square and/ or Piccadilly Circus, the footfall of people viewing your image is immense, so your fee will be – should be! – commensurate.

Editorial and magazine shoots aren't as well paid because these guys are shooting every week. These fees could be anything from £100 to £500 a day. E-commerce fees are very similar to regular commercial day fees and can range from £400 to £800 per day.

Agency fees

All agencies make money from charging a fee on commercial jobs. The fee is charged on the whole fee to the model, so you should familiarise yourself with the fee your agency charges.

---

12   https://www.thinkbox.tv

This varies from agent to agent: from around 10–15% for acting agencies dealing with long film bookings, to around 30% for model agencies booking stills shoots. Model agencies on average charge a third of the whole fee, with VAT added to all fees. Castings are not paid as they are like interviews, but most other things are paid for by the client, such as the following:

- **Recall fee:** The second requested 'recall' casting, mainly for TV commercials and film work rather than stills (usually the fee will be enough to cover expenses).
- **Travel day:** For example, if you are travelling abroad, as this is a whole day out when you might otherwise have booked another job. The fee will be half the day fee.
- **Rest day:** Normally the same as the travel day fee. This would be paid if a model were on a shoot abroad and is not shooting that day – maybe the team are scouting and the model isn't needed.
- **Shoot day fee, studio fee or basic studio fee (BSF):** This is the fee for the actual shoot day. The usage fee might sometimes be part of the shoot day fee, so do ask your agent.
- **Usage fee:** There is sometimes a usage fee on top of the shoot day fee. This is negotiated according to the reach of the images. The usage fee is due as soon as the images or footage go live.
- **Travel:** These costs are covered for most jobs for which you have to travel (so the train/bus/taxi fare, or mileage if you are driving), unless otherwise negotiated with the client beforehand.

Confirmation forms

When you've been booked on a shoot (well done, you!), your

agency will send a confirmation form to the client so that everyone is clear on who is being booked for what job. The form will include all the details of the job, including the booking terms of business. If you don't have an agent, you should email a confirmation form to the client yourself. Details should include:

- Client details.
- Project.
- Usage.
- Location.
- Health-and-safety requirements.
- Expenses.
- Invoicing details
- Model name.
- Rate.
- Time and date of booking.
- Total rates (including/excluding VAT).

This section might be a little dry, but it's essential to have every piece of information, and to understand that, as a model, you are entering into a legal contract with the client. You also need to ensure that your health and well-being are maintained at all times. You need to be protected.

Working hours

Stills shoots are based on an eight-hour working day, Monday to Friday, from 9am until 5pm. Film shoots are based on a ten-hour working day; this is because moving images are more involved in terms of lighting and sets. For stills shoots, a booking of over five hours is classed as a whole day. Half-day rates are based on a four-hour booking. Overtime is payable for time worked over the eight-hour day. As a rule, over half an hour past the ninth hour is overtime. Special rates should be agreed for weekends, bank holidays and night shoots. Film shoot days are longer at ten hours, with potential overtime rates negotiated beforehand. A longer shoot day will usually be flagged before the shoot to avoid any surprises on the day of the shoot.

Exclusivity fees are complicated. If a client wants a model to be the face of their brand only, and no other client to use their face, an exclusivity deal will be struck. For the model, this could be a double-edged sword. On the one hand you will be able to command a lucrative fee to work with that brand alone. On the other, if the campaign is worldwide, you will only be associated with that one brand, and when the contract has finished, you will have to work very hard to dissociate yourself from that client and obtain work with other clients and competitors.

I have two examples. I knew a model who was booked for a campaign selling a cold-sore product. The ad was *everywhere*! Billboards, TV, magazines, online, flyers… And because the model was associated with that brand only, she didn't work for a long time after the campaign because everyone regarded her as 'the cold-sore model'. Another (well-known) model was booked for a campaign for an insurance company. Again, the campaign was *massive*! Billboards, TV, magazines…the lot. I bumped into her at a casting, and she told me that she didn't get booked for anything else because of her association with that insurance company. Thankfully, she managed to sidestep into TV presenting and has gone on to carve out a fabulous career…perfect!

Semi-exclusive deals are also possible. This is when a model is booked exclusively within a particular sector only, such as holiday companies. The contract allows them to work for other clients in all other sectors aside from holidays. Semi-exclusive contracts aren't as lucrative, but are worth having nonetheless.

Cancellation fees

Cancellation fees are a minefield, so let me make this as simple as possible for you. If your job is cancelled within twenty-four hours of a booking, the whole fee should be paid unless you are rebooked within that same twenty-four-hour period, in which case, half the fee should be paid. If the shoot has to be postponed due to the weather, generally there should be some flexibility from both sides.

When the global Covid-19 pandemic struck in March 2020, the entire modelling industry was brought to its knees. Unsurprisingly, modelling requires person-to-person contact, so the first six months of the pandemic were fraught, to say the least. Like most industries, the modelling world hadn't experienced anything like it before, and no one was immune. At Gingersnap, we went from ten shoots a day to nothing but cancellations across the board. Fortunately for the model industry, the world required the television industry to quickly navigate a path towards reopening shoots, with PCR and rapid lateral flow tests, and self-isolating before shoots. As I write this, things have, thankfully, settled down and returned to some degree of normality, but the scars remain and there are far more relaxed cancellation terms when the reasons are Covid related.

Meals

Meals should be provided by the client on the day of the shoot, taking into account any dietary requirements. When you join an agency, you should be asked if you have any specific dietary needs.

Model care and safety

The health and well-being of models on shoots should always be maintained. The venue should be safe and secure to allow the model to provide a service in compliance with all health-and-safety standards, regulations, codes and laws. There should be regular rest periods – given that there is usually a lot of waiting around at shoots, this should come naturally!

The client should have insurance cover to safeguard health and safety. Recently, we dealt with an unfortunate case in which a model's skin was burned by a hair-and-make-up artist's curling irons. As the model's agent, we at Gingersnap requested insurance documents from the client/hair-and-make-up artist and submitted them to the model because she couldn't work for a few weeks with the burn on her face. This doesn't happen a lot, but it's something a model should be aware of. The client should also ensure that the team working with the models are suitably qualified, experienced and professional. No one should impose upon the model any action or activity which is dangerous, degrading, unprofessional or demeaning. This reminds me of a model I met soon after I started Gingersnap. During the course of our conversation, the poor girl got really upset when she began telling me about an encounter she had experienced the week before. She had turned up to what she thought was a model casting (not booked through an agent, I hasten to add) and unwittingly found herself in one of Europe's largest porn studios. She went into the casting and the first thing they asked her for was her HIV certificate.[13] She had no idea what she was walking into, and certainly no interest in the porn industry, so she hotfooted it out of there!

In theory, on any shoot the client should provide a private changing/dressing area. However, in reality it's not always possible. Believe me when I say that on many shoots I have changed in the toilets. I guess it's private! As a model you must be prepared to change (quickly!) in any given corner – on the

13   An HIV certificate, apparently, is a document proving that you do not have HIV.

street, in alleyways, in a cold warehouse…you name it, I have changed there.

Intellectual property rights

The photographer or client is not entitled to use any images beyond the agreed or permitted use. The agency (or you if you don't have an agent) is the licence holder of all commercial and intellectual property rights relating to the model. Clients are not entitled to exploit, or enter into any commercial agreement to exploit, any rights relating to models' images. Please remember that the actual image rights always belong to the photographer. Look at the photographer as the artist owning the work created with their camera. The model's images in terms of usage of *where* the images are being used is controlled by the model agent (or model if not agency represented.) Hard to get your head around, I know.

Sorting Your Head Out

On the 13 February 2007, eighteen-year-old Uruguayan model Eliana Ramos was found dead in her bed by her grandma. She had died of a heart attack that was later found to be linked to anorexia nervosa. For any family this would be tragic, but for the Ramoses it was a shocking case of lightning striking twice. Unfathomably, Eliana's elder sister and fellow model Luisel had also collapsed and died in her dressing room after a fashion show just six months previously. She was twenty-two, and her death was also linked to anorexia.

After the deaths of the Ramos sisters, there was an outcry in the modelling industry in an attempt to change the way in which models were treated in terms of their bodies and mental health. The Italian and French governments passed laws preventing size zero models from working in fashion weeks. Today, French clients ban models with a body mass index (BMI) of under eighteen from working. French models should be in possession of a medical certificate from a designated health professional declaring them to have a healthy BMI and be fit enough to work. Additionally, agencies that use models without valid medical certification can face a fine of €75,000, while staff can be sentenced to up to six months in prison. Failure to flag up retouched images will incur a fine of €37,500, or up to 30% of the amount spent on the advert.

In 2007, the British Fashion Council convened a panel of leading experts including psychologists, designers, models, model agencies and health professionals to submit a timely report, *Fashioning a Healthy Future: The Report of the Model Health Inquiry*. Its main contributors were the BFC and the Association of Model Agents (AMA). I was one of the contributors to the report, and it made for an interesting read. It contained research on what was happening in 2007, in terms of models' mental health. Compiled after interviewing working models and taking on board the views of designers and mental health professionals, it listed a number of suggested changes to improve the industry:

- Additional support for models aged sixteen to eighteen, including chaperones where appropriate.
- A ban on under-sixteens being used in London Fashion Week (LFW) shows.
- Criminal Records Bureau (CRB) checks for model agents, designers, photographers and casting directors who deal with child models: "The fashion industry should be in line with other sectors working with children."

These suggestions are industry-changing ones and would mean that young models were not so vulnerable. To the industry's shame, however, nothing was done. In an ironic (given the industry) spot of window dressing, the report garnered some good press and painted the BFC in a positive light, but nothing was acted upon. To make real changes, real laws will need to be passed.

As the mother of three girls, a former model and a professional model agent, the potential changes were music to my ears. As young models in the '90s, we were lined up in our pants and bras and measured in the toilets every month. The bookers would stand at the end of the line with their clipboards, measuring every inch of us. Models had to be the 'ideal' size or be cast out of the agency, so there was a lot of pressure. As a skinny girl from Taunton, I would stare in bewilderment as 'Sarah' (name changed), another of my housemates in the agency flat, recounted to me every morsel she had eaten, explaining in detail the juice plan she was undertaking in the hope of becoming the skinniest model at the next measuring session. "I want to be skinny so I can be the most successful model possible," she would say. "This is what I've always wanted, and now I'm with the top agency in London, nothing will get in my way!"

Two months later, as I was coming into the agency building, Sarah burst out of the lift, in floods of tears and with make-up sliding down her face. "Sarah, what's happened?" I asked.

"I've been thrown out. That's it," she replied in utter devastation. "Apparently, I'm too fat for the agency and they can't represent me any more. They've told me I need to move out of the agency flat tonight because someone else is moving in."

Sarah was broken. But that was the reality of modelling in the 1990s: there was an inordinate amount of pressure from designers requiring size zero models for their sample sizes. If you didn't get the shows, you weren't booked for the editorials. If you weren't booked for the editorials, you didn't get any huge campaigns that would bring money to the agency, so you were useless.

Thank the Lord the industry is a kinder place today. Plus-size models earn more than ever before; model differences are celebrated, not mocked; and there's a place in the industry for anyone who wants to jump in.

Model and actress Cara Delevingne suffered from depression. On the breakfast show *This Morning* she talked about liking her image, or the person she thought she was, but hating her real self. She reached a breakdown point, and told the presenters, "I had depression and I had moments where I didn't want to carry on living. And then the guilt of feeling that way and not being able to tell anyone, because I shouldn't feel that way and shouldn't feel bad... Don't give in to what people think about you, and just follow your dreams. You can achieve anything!"[14]

There's no doubt about it: modelling messes with your head. We are working in an industry which breeds anxiety and creates insecurities. We often deal with people at an extremely vulnerable time in their lives – many of our models start between sixteen to eighteen years old, which is such a fragile time psychologically and physically. Your body is changing; you're growing up and having to reconcile yourself to being an adult emerging into a constantly changing world. It really isn't an easy time. Social media has a lot to answer for, too. Beautiful images and beautiful bodies, smiles and giggles, sunsets, sunrises and wonderful lives all on show. Insta model, Insta famous, Insta life. You don't even need to be a model; with filters at your fingertips, anyone can look like they have the perfect life, face, body and world. The only difference is that real models don't need as much Facetuning.

Well, let's put down the phone for a sec and have a look at what's really happening here.

What's the story, morning glory?

Let's start with the crazy early mornings. I worked a lot in Miami, shooting German catalogues. The German catalogue market was *huge*! There used to be lots of teams shooting twice a year all over the world, but mainly in Miami and South Africa, where you are promised beautiful sunrises and amazing locations.

---

14   Cara Delevingne, *This Morning* interview, 9 October 2017.

To catch the right light, you must be up with the lark! Don't forget that you might have flown in the day before, so you are pretty jet-lagged too. You set your alarm for 4am. You should be ready – showered and with dried, fresh hair – in the location van by 4.30, and the drive to the location can take up to an hour, with your hair and make-up being done on the way. By 5.30 you are dressed in your first outfit and on set, shooting. Catalogue modelling is about selling the clothes. You have to 'cheat' poses so that your body might feel uncomfortable, but from the front the clothes look amazing. The photographer could be quite a way down the beach with a long lens to capture both you and the location, so you'd better be on your toes! There is usually a radio link between the set and the photographer so they can speak to you about what looks great and what doesn't. You're constantly on the move so that each shot is different from the one before, all the while hoping that the money shot comes quickly as you know you have twenty outfits to get through before the sun is too high for the shoot to continue. You finish around 11am and then get back to the hotel, where you get some rest until you all meet again at 3pm to do the sunset light.

I used to go months working like this, all over the world. You get very tired and very lonely.

Are you lonesome tonight?

Right, let's get inside your head and talk you, you and more you. You are a self-employed model who can only work alone. There's only one you, so you might as well get to know and learn to love yourself and your own company. It's always hard as a young model, watching other models around you succeed. I remember standing in newsagent's stores, looking through all the mags, seeing all my peers and thinking, Why not me? I guess today's equivalent are the various social media platforms: Instagram,

Facebook and TikTok. Looking back, what I really wanted was a hug from behind and a whisper in my ear from my forty-nine-year-old self. It would have been a strong, safe bear hug with both arms, and I would have said, "Don't worry – your time will come! You may have to wait, but it *will* come, Clare!" You must believe me when I say that if you work hard enough at something you really want, you can and will succeed. It might not be in the way you originally thought, but I promise you that hard work and determination pay off.

By the way, I spoke to Sarah a few years ago and she was deliriously happy working as a model booker. She is working in her dream job and living her best life!

I say no, no, no!

According to a 2020 survey undertaken by the University of Ulster, it's estimated that two thirds of those working in the creative industries have had suicidal thoughts. The same survey discovered that if you work in fashion, you are 25% more likely to suffer from a mental illness. I reckon that's pretty high odds, but we are not alone. There are definitely other industries dominated by professionals which have similarly high occurrences of mental health issues – namely jockeys, wrestlers and athletes, alongside us models, actors and ballet dancers. The *Fashioning a Healthy Future* report (2007) called them 'at risk populations'. It is the issue of body weight which binds these groups, coupled with the constant fear of rejection if weight gets out of control. Most of these careers offer incredible accolades and are mainly occupied by youngsters, so there's little wonder the stress levels involved are high.

Under pressure

There's no denying it: the modelling industry is filled with all

91

ages of people, the majority are young. Many are desperate to 'make it big' in any way possible. I was desperate to get away from the place where I grew up. For me, home was an unhappy place. I didn't fit in. London's alluring bright lights beckoned. Modelling offered me another life; one in which I had to succeed. Put simply, in my mind there was no other option.

I was sixteen when I first arrived in the capital in the summer of 1989; a new model with the acclaimed Models 1. This was going to be the best summer of my life. I was young and free. For the first few weeks I was doing tests and travelling across London, seeing photographers, magazines and clients, with up to ten meetings on most days. Back then, models' health and safety weren't really 'a thing'. There were so many models, and opportunities flying in every direction. Many times, I found myself in situations which were quite questionable. I was naive, from the back end of Somerset, and had no idea what was right and what was wrong within the industry.

On one occasion, I agreed to do a test with a photographer. He let me into his apartment, and it was just me and him. He was wearing a huge pair of baggy green Y-fronts, and dirty Adidas trainers on his feet. We went to his bedroom, where he said, "I just need you in your pants on my bed."

I didn't even think about it. I took everything off and put it in a pile beside the bed whilst he removed his shoes. My booker's voice was ringing through my head: "I'm so excited you're doing this test, babe. It's going to be so good for your book – this photographer is bloody amazing, darling!" I had to be professional. This was all above board; it was going to be okay.

I lay on the bed whilst the photographer sorted his camera. He told me that he was going to shoot everything from above. He jumped on the bed and straddled my body with his feet; then he touched my thigh with one bare foot. "Move," he demanded from behind the camera.

I looked at him apprehensively, my face screaming, Erm... what is it you want me to do? But the words would not come out of my mouth. I was a sixteen-year-old girl from the backwaters of Taunton – a world away from how things worked in London. I was inexperienced, not to mention confused. I tried to be professional and get into the vibe he wanted.

The test was an hour long and I left soon after. When the pictures came back, the agency was so excited. They made a new card out of them, and got new prints for my book. The pictures were great, but that feeling of vulnerability will never leave me. The model industry is a creative one, therefore attracts some questionable characters. Looking back, I was too young to differentiate between creativity and eccentricity. In the end I chalked it all down to lack of experience. Young models should be treated carefully.

To be clear, no abuse happened that day – not in the physical sense, at least. But – and this is critical – the situation felt inappropriate. I should have been chaperoned, as would later be suggested in the *Fashioning a Healthy Future* report, but those changes have still not been made, and will not be made any time soon.

Therefore, for the time being, the answer lies with the models themselves. If you find yourself in a vulnerable situation, call your agent immediately and they will sort it out. Photographers and clients are all vetted by agencies, but be warned: where there are young models, there are always potential predators. The best advice I can think of is to work hard whilst you can and stay safe and healthy. Make the most of it, take it seriously, do the job to the best of your ability, raise any concerns you have, give it your best shot and you'll have no regrets.

Better to try and fail than not to try at all.
(William F O'Brien)

It's very easy for me to sit here and write, 'Learn to love "no".' But when you're the person getting rejected, it's hard. I know; I've been there. As a model or an actor, you soon get to know if clients are interested in you. Their body language changes. They become warmer. They start telling you about the job: the start dates, other people involved. They ask you questions about yourself and other jobs you've done. You just get a good feeling about the shoot. Sometimes you get a run of people booking you, and it feels great. Of course it does! However, there is a flip side. At other times it feels like everyone apart from you is getting booked. It can get harder and harder to bounce back after each rejection. Sometimes it can feel exhausting, being pulled and pushed by the constant tide of other people's decisions.

I was about twenty and had been modelling for four years when things suddenly clicked into place. And guess what? You totally have some influence over whether you are booked or not, and this is how: use a touch of reverse psychology. No one likes to hear bad or sad news, and everyone likes to hear about good stuff. So, here's my five-point plan to nail that casting:

1. Dress in clothes you feel confident and badass wearing, whilst keeping in mind the job brief...so long as you look and feel *great*!

2. Chat to clients like you already have the job. They want to see the most confident and natural version of you.

3. Hold your head high and immediately you will look and feel confident in your own skin. Remember not to fidget or show any sign that you could be nervous – you've got this!

4. Psychologically channel the most iconic person you

can think of: Beyoncé, Kim Kardashian, Nicki Minaj, Gemma Collins…

5. Only talk about the jobs you have booked recently. Make them sound bigger and better. If you did a little feature, it's the magazine, whether it's a feature or not. If you are doing a social media post for a brand, you are working for the brand. Doing a test with a photographer? You are working with that photographer… Get the idea? We are bending the truth a touch to make your work sound as fabulous as we can. No one else is going to beef you up apart from your agency. I guess it's like verbal Instagram posts.

It took me four years of being in the industry to realise that positive stories sell you. As soon as this clicked, my work changed beyond recognition. I went from working a day every few weeks, to working most days. When clients can't book a model because they're working other jobs, they want them even more. Believe me, you'll get busy. This approach works like a dream.

There are other simple steps that you can take to stay positive as well as maintain your mental health:

Mode Magazine, photographer Steve Shaw

- Take time away from devices and social media.

- Get a good night's sleep.
- Book some time off work.
- Speak to a friend or your family about your feelings.
- Take some exercise: run, dance, go to the gym or practise yoga.
- Meditate! Sit calmly and take slow breaths to ease anxiety.

If none of these work, you should speak to a health professional who can advise you on the next steps.

Mental health support

Believe it or not, there are currently no websites or contacts which offer mental health support specifically for models.

All reputable agencies should offer guidance and support on well-being including for mental health. Gingersnap has a model handbook which informs new models on many issues including mental health. Reputable agencies should also have paperwork running alongside their contracts that offers guidance. I would advise asking for as much information as possible when you first join the agency.

Despite the glamour associated with modelling, it can be quite a lonely

Mode Magazine,
photographer Steve Shaw

experience. The Be Well Collective[15] is a great organisation that offers coaching and mental health support for models and others in the creative industries. I wish they had been there when I first started modelling.

Some other mental health organisations include:

- **Mind**: https://www.mind.org.uk/
- **YoungMinds**: https://www.youngminds.org.uk/
- **The Mental Health Foundation**: https://www.mentalhealth.org.uk/
- **The Prince's Trust**: http://www.princes-trust.org/help-for-young-people/who-else/housing-health-wellbeing/wellbeing/mental-health

---

15   https://www.bewellcollective.co.uk

Baby and Child Modelling

Child modelling can lead to an incredible long-term career in many different fields. Some of Hollywood's biggest names were borne out of the modelling circuit:

- **Cameron Diaz** started modelling aged sixteen. She travelled all over the world on the modelling circuit before landing the main female part in *The Mask*. I spent a week with her in 1993, just as Cameron had finished filming. We were both booked for a British catalogue shoot in Arizona. The blonde British model who was originally booked didn't turn up at the airport, so Cameron was flown over from LA to replace her. She was a lovely, regular, and high-spirited American model. She told me she'd been modelling for quite a few years, and had recently done "this little movie called *The Mask* a few months back". I don't think she or anyone else had a clue how famous she would become off the back of that film. A few months later, I was back at university, writing an essay with the TV on, and I heard her familiar voice and immediately looked up and smiled. Go on, Cameron!

- **Robert Pattinson** modelled from the ages of twelve to sixteen before he was picked up by an acting agent.

- **Brad Pitt** modelled for a huge Levi's commercial.

- **Angelina Jolie** modelled during high school.

- **Jennifer Lawrence** modelled on the side for years

until her acting career took off.

- **Lindsay Lohan** started modelling at the age of three. She shot over sixty different commercials!
- **Channing Tatum** modelled for Armani, Dolce & Gabbana, and Abercrombie & Fitch.
- **Kirsten Dunst** started modelling for children's fashion companies at the age of three.
- **Amanda Seyfried** modelled for a book cover for the kids' book series *Sweet Valley High*.
- **Ashton Kutcher** did many catwalk shows before his acting career took off.
- **Gwyneth Paltrow** did teen modelling (including a campaign about condoms, which is still online).
- **Reese Witherspoon** started in the industry as a child model.
- **Charlize Theron** was a bra model before she was an actor.
- **Jamie Dornan** shot with Kate Moss in 2005.
- **Keeley Hawes** modelled while her acting was still in the background. We were both represented by Models 1, and used to tramp all over London to castings and have a right old laugh on the Tubes and buses. She is a lovely, down-to-earth lady and we had lots of fun together.
- There are, of course, current models too who started when they were young girls – **Gigi Hadid** and **Karlie Kloss** are two examples who are still huge names on the circuit.

Hollywood fame can be lucrative and marvellous, but it's not everyone's bag. Take a look behind the scenes, and for each person in front of the camera, there's a whole host of crew standing there, playing important roles. Plenty of successful models have gone on to follow careers on the other side of the camera.

Modelling as a youngster opens your eyes to an exciting, creative world; one that can be equally addictive and rewarding. I have met many film directors, producers, photographers, make-up and hair artists, agents, artists and musicians who have a background in modelling. Personally, I didn't ever crave to be in front of the film cameras. I had plenty of castings for huge films, including one with Stanley Kubrick for *Eyes Wide Shut* with Tom Cruise and Nicole Kidman. It was the perfect opportunity, but I wanted to be behind, not in front of, the lens! To be a great actor is in the blood, and you need to want it more than anything else in the world. I used to stare at the producers and clients on their mobile phones, wheeling and dealing all day long, organising the next day's shoots, locations and models, negotiating various problems, and think to myself, Yeah, that's where I want to be after modelling. I want to be the one with the phone!

One of the greatest things about the creative industries is that sidestepping into other areas is very achievable. Once you make the contacts, it's all about networking to morph yourself into what you want to be. The industry is full of photographers who used to be models, models who used to be photographers, make-up artists who used to be models, agents who used to be models (including me!), and so on...

It's the greatest compliment when someone says that your child is beautiful, talented or clever. Confirmation of that compliment arrives when that child is chosen to be a model. As an agency, Gingersnap gets thousands of child applications every month but, just like adults, not all children can be professional models.

There are a few things that need to be considered before

taking those first 'baby steps' into the modelling world:

- **Confidence:** Can your child walk into a room and talk to anyone? Studios are very large spaces, filled mainly with adults. In that space, many crew members including your child, are being paid quite a lot of money to be there. Money means pressure, and pressure can mean stress and worry. If your child is a wallflower who shrinks in a stranger's presence, this world is not for them. If you have a confident chappie on your hands who can soon relax in an unfamiliar environment, modelling could very well be their thing. All children can be shy at first, but the best child models are the ones who warm up fast and know that they are there to get in front of the camera and take direction well.

- **Time and money:** As your child's legal chaperone, you should be prepared to give up your time to take them to shoots and stay at the studio for the whole day. Lindsay Lohan, Kirsten Dunst, Robert Pattinson, Gwyneth Paltrow, Reese Witherspoon, Keeley Hawes…there's no doubting that they all had very understanding and patient parents (or grandparents) waiting in the wings for shoot days to end. If you are happy to have a flexible work schedule and can afford to wait around in a studio for days on end to support your child model, all good. Bear in mind too that you will need childcare for any other children you have. It is frowned upon to take siblings to a shoot. For the client it means more mouths to feed, and more worry in terms of insurance and health-and-safety considerations. Modelling is a professional job, and the only child who attends should be the one who has been booked. As a successful model, I'd say I was booked following 10–20% of the castings I went for, and this is a high percentage! I was a redhead too, so my work was very niche. Think of all the castings you are going to take your child to. If you live outside the city where the casting is happening, that's maybe two to three hours' driving or train journey each way. Castings are prospective meetings, so the travel costs are paid by you, the parent.

- **Managing expectations:** Let's get real about castings. There are a whole host of similar-looking child models and actors in line with their parents, waiting to be seen by the photographer, director and/or production team. It is the casting director's job to narrow down the list to a few possible options for each role, so there will be many children like your own, all going for the same part. Manage both your child's and your own expectations. Children should be made to feel positive about the casting. If you are feeling like the past three hours in the car getting there have been in vain because you are tenth in the queue behind some very good-looking options for the same role, hide it. Be upbeat and positive. If nothing else, your child is about to get in front of some industry professionals who will give them something very valuable: *experience*! And remember, while they might not be successful in bagging one role, there could well be others in other productions they'll be considered for. You have some influence over how your child is presented, how they get to the casting, and what they say and do while there. You do not have any control over what the director has in mind for the role. If your child fits what is required on the day, you have a chance. Read the casting brief and the script from the agency carefully. Get your child into the role by going through what they will be doing in the casting so it's not a huge shock. Everyone has a chance, but the more organised you are, the greater your child's chances. Remain positive!

- **Adaptability:** As an agent, I don't get anyone excited about a role unless they have been 100% confirmed. I tell parents to downplay any job that is pencilled in with their child until it's a sure thing. It's an unfortunate fact that clients are notorious for changing their minds about castings. Schedules, weather, other models and actors, scripts and situations can always change. Many stars have to align before a confirmation, so keep your cool! There is one irrefutable thing you can take as gospel in this industry: things almost always happen at the last minute. Professional models should be prepared to drop most (non-life-threatening!) things for a booking. Please tell your child's agents when you have holidays booked, because on most working days good agencies will be working on getting your child bookings, so they need to be in the know. Models who are on tap will get booked a lot by their agency because they know you are keen and will not let them down. One thing is certain: once you string along an agent with a load of excuses, they won't work as hard for you again, so keep the excuses legitimate!

Getting your child an agent

Companies who use images of children only go through model agencies to book their kids. Next, Zara, M&S, Gap, Disney and other holidays parks, Mattel, Trunki – you name it, they will only deal with agencies. Why? Because they're guaranteed to get vetted and experienced models. Professional agencies put models through rigorous testing processes before they are put forward to paying clients.

So how do you get your child an agent? There are many agencies out there. Your first step should be to look online. I just googled 'child model agencies' and there are quite a few lists you can access.[16] Once you have your list, look at each agency's website and have a nosy around their Instagram. What you are looking for is a list of paying clients they work with (Gap, Next, M&S…). If you can't see any evidence of shoots, call the agency and speak to the bookers about the kind of clients they work with. If they start talking about you paying them any money or a deposit, run in the opposite direction. Real agencies make their money from the commission they get from booking models on shoots, after they have invested time in taking on those models.

Child licences

Every child under sixteen who is being paid for any kind of performance, including shoots and theatre, must hold a child performance licence. The agency and client will sort the licence for you, and will ask for some paperwork which they will present to your local council:

- Child's birth certificate.
- Part 2 application form (the parents' section of the application form).
- Medical declaration confirming the child's state of health.
- Permission letter from the child's school if they are of school age.

16   This list looks great, but just try to ensure that you get an up-to-date one as agencies are always changing names and contact details: https://www.juniormagazine.co.uk/fashion/10-of-the-best-child-model-agencies

More information on licensing can be found on the government website.[17]

The client also needs to carry out due diligence when working with children. Here's an example of a child protection policy which every client has to complete before working with children:

Gingersnap Modelling Agency
Child Protection Policy

At Gingersnap Modelling Agency, the welfare of children is paramount, and every child should have a positive experience.

This Child Protection Policy is to promote good practice of protecting children with appropriate safety whilst they are in the care of Gingersnap Modelling Agency.

Everyone working with children must know how to treat children and how to act around children in order to protect them whilst they are in our care.

All children have a right to protection. This Policy refers to all children under the age of 18.

All children, whatever their age, culture, disability, gender, language spoken, racial origin, religious beliefs and/or sexual identity, have the right to protection from abuse.

All suspicions and allegations of abuse/mistreatment will be taken seriously and responded to swiftly and appropriately. Everyone working for the Photographer has a responsibility to report concerns to the appropriate person.

CONTACTS
info@gingersnap.co.uk
01179294450

---

17   https://www.gov.uk/apply-for-child-performance-licence

1. BEHAVIOUR

- Gingersnap Modelling Agency expects adults (being staff, parents/guardians, chaperones and anyone else who comes into contact with children) to behave in an appropriate manner at all times. The welfare of all children is the adult's responsibility regardless of their role. Adults are expected to:
    - Be friendly and polite.
    - Introduce all the children to staff and to all other children on set.
    - Make children welcome and familiar with their environment.
    - Inform children of where the toilets are, where the fire exits are, what to do in the case of an emergency, and any health-and-safety information.
    - Let children know who the appropriate person is to speak to should they have any questions or concerns.
- When filming, please remember that children need to be treated differently from adults.
- It is helpful for the staff to stay positive, i.e. give enthusiastic and constructive feedback rather than negative criticism. If you are positive and patient, you will always get the best out of a child.
    - If necessary, allow a child a five-minute break to practise or rest if they are finding something difficult – this can help with their nerves and their concentration.

1.1 CHILDREN'S BEHAVIOUR

- We do not usually have problems with children's

behaviour. However, if a child is repeatedly being disruptive or misbehaving, please speak to the child's parent/guardian/chaperone to warn them that if the behaviour continues, they will be asked to leave.

- Some behaviour may be due to excitement or nerves so please make allowances for this.

- Reprimanding children should always be done in private, away from other children but preferably in front of the child's parent/guardian/chaperone. No harsh words should be used and you should never aim to bring the child to tears.

2.   CHILD WELFARE

2.1   SUPERVISION

- Each child needs to be supervised *at all times*. They should be with their parent/guardian/chaperone when travelling to and from the shoot, whilst on set or in the green room or changing rooms, at mealtimes, and when going to the toilet.

    - Children MUST arrive accompanied by a parent, guardian or chaperone.

    - If a child arrives alone or with an older child, they will not be allowed to participate. The child's parent/guardian/chaperone or Agency will be contacted and told to collect the child at a mutually agreed time, but usually no longer than an hour later. If the parent/guardian/chaperone does not arrive at the agreed time, you will need to contact social services and inform the producer on set.

- You MUST NOT let the child leave on their own – no

matter how old they are, even if they arrived on their own.

- If a child arrives with an adult other than their parent/guardian/chaperone, the Photographer must have had prior written consent from the child's parent/guardian/chaperone for such adult to bring the child along. There must be a licensed chaperone who will be responsible for that child whilst they are at the studio/location.

- The council need a copy of the chaperone's licence for every chaperone prior to the chaperone being hired. This is the responsibility of whoever is hiring the child.

- Each child MUST BE LICENSED. It is the responsibility of the person who is hiring the child to ensure that the child is licensed.

2.2   DBS CHECKS

- All Gingersnap Modelling Agency's employees who are regularly working with children will be DBS cleared (Disclosure and Barring Service).

- If you have any queries concerning this matter, then please talk to the HR Department.

2.3   SUSPECTED ABUSE

- Any bruising, scratches, repeated flinching or any other form of excessively timid behaviour that you believe could be caused by the child being abused MUST be reported to the producer on set.

- If a child confides in you that he/she is being abused, you will need to contact the producer on set, who will take it forward.

- You will also need to complete the attached Child Incident Report form for EVERY child incident.

- PLEASE REMEMBER that abuse and bullying are sensitive issues and should therefore be dealt with confidentially.

2.4   BULLYING

- Bullying will not be accepted in any form or by anyone.
- If you suspect a child is being bullied by a parent/ guardian/chaperone, please speak to them immediately in private, away from the child, and ask them to stop. Warn them that if it continues, they and the child will be asked to leave. If the bullying continues, please ensure that they leave promptly and with the minimum of fuss.
- Examples of bullying by a parent/guardian/chaperone are:
    - Humiliating the child.
    - Putting too much pressure on the child.
    - Being too pushy.
    - Upsetting the child in any way.
- If you believe a member of staff is bullying a child, please speak to them in private and point out what they are doing – they may not realise that their behaviour is not acceptable. Warn them that if it continues, you will speak to the producer on set, who will take further action.
- If a child is bullying another child, please speak to their parent/guardian/chaperone, who should speak to them and ask them to stop. They should also be warned that if the bullying continues, they will be asked to leave and will not be asked back again by Gingersnap Modelling Agency. This should be enough of a deterrent.
- Please also record any form of bullying you see,

whoever is doing it, using the Child Incident Report form attached.

2.5   FOOD

- The children must be provided with snacks during shoots, e.g. fruit and biscuits.
- If a child is filming with Gingersnap Modelling Agency for four hours or more, snacks and a suitable meal must be provided – usually sandwiches.
- If a child is filming all day, a hot meal must be provided as well as two snack breaks.
- Meals must be provided if the children are filming over a mealtime, even if they are only filming for two hours.
- Children have a high metabolism, and to get the best out of them, you need to ensure that they have regular food and water. They must only be filming for an hour and a half maximum before having a snack break.
- Generally, if a child attends a morning shoot, breakfast should be supplied, and for afternoon shoots, afternoon tea should be supplied.
- Bottled water must be available all day and juice must be provided at break times.
- Please avoid fizzy drinks for the children.
- Gingersnap Modelling Agency has a policy to promote a healthy lifestyle – please remember this when buying food for the children.
- All food must be purchased on the day and stored within health-and-safety guidelines.
- If a child has a food allergy, is a vegan/vegetarian, or does not eat certain foods for religious reasons, please ask parents/guardians to provide a packed lunch for their child as we cannot guarantee being able to

purchase suitable foods for these children.

- Please also ensure that each parent/guardian has duly completed and signed an Allergy and Medication form as attached and provided it to the Photographer in advance.

2.6   BREAKS

- Children obviously need a lot more breaks than adults. Please see the following chart regarding the minimum legal requirements for breaks.
- However, depending on the nature of the work and the children involved, it may be necessary to give additional breaks.

	Age 0–4	Age 5–8	Age 9 & over
Maximum Time at place of Performance	5 Hours	7 Hours	9 Hours
Maximum Time Present	Between 9.30am & 4.30pm	Between 9am & 4.30pm	Between 7am & 7pm
Maximum Performing Time	2 Hours	3 Hours	4 Hours
Maximum continuous time to take part without a rest	30 Minutes	45 Minutes	1 Hour

Maximum Rest/Meal Times	All times when not taking part	Present 3½ Hours = 2 breaks, 1 Hour Meal and 15 mins rest	Present 4 Hours = 2 breaks, 2 x 1 Hour meal and 15 mins rest
Education	NIL	3 Hours per school day (see Education for aggregated hours)	3 Hours per school day (see Education for aggregated hours)

Exceptions: BBC/ITV and Contractors or children aged 13 and over only (Ref 27 (2)(a))

Maximum time 7-day week

12 Hours any 1 day **OR** 9 Hours any 33 days provided not present on any other day that week and not present after 7pm on max. 20 days in previous 12 months

Times between 7am & 7pm **OR** between 10am & 10pm

ALTERNATIVE TO ABOVE EXCEPTIONS (Ref 27(2)(b))

Maximum time 7-day week

12 Hours 1 day provided not present more than 4 hours any other day that week and does not take part on the day following on which they were present after 7pm and has not been present after 7pm on any of the 6 previous days.

Times between 7am & 7pm **OR** between 10am and 10pm

2.7 ALLERGIES AND MEDICATION

- If a child has an allergy, the parents need to inform us in advance of this, in writing, explaining the allergy and possible reaction in detail.

- If a child suffers from a skin condition, they may not be able to use gunge as they could suffer an adverse reaction.
- Only the child, or his or her parent/guardian/chaperone, is allowed to administer any medication the child may need whilst on set.
- Please ensure all parents complete an Allergy and Medication form in advance.

2.8   CHANGING AND WASHING FACILITIES

- There must be NO sharing of changing rooms – one for boys, one for girls and one for adults. [At the time of writing, this may be subject to change.]
- If there is a large age gap between children then two boys' and two girls' changing rooms would need to be considered, or for different ages to change at different times.
- If there is limited space, then the same changing rooms can be used by boys, girls and adults, but at different times. This needs to be made very clear to everyone involved.
- No adults may enter the changing rooms unless a child needs help. If a child does need help then they must go in separately from all the other children.
- Children of certain ages may not want to dress/undress in front of other children – please make allowances for this.

2.9   AGE OF CHILDREN

- It is important to ensure that when working with children you consider the age of the children concerned – toddlers have very different needs to teenagers. For example, a toddler will not have as large a vocabulary or understand as much as a teenager.

- Another point to remember is that some children may feel uncomfortable wearing certain clothing or taking part in some activities as their bodies develop, and they may not want to discuss the reasons why. Please try to be very sensitive to these issues.

2.10   COSTUMES

- It is important to see things from a child's point of view. Children are all different shapes and sizes, and any clothing/costumes must take this into account.

2.11   SICKNESS AND TIREDNESS

- As soon as a child begins to feel unwell, they must leave the set immediately with their parent/guardian/chaperone and a Child Incident Report form must be completed.
- If a child is accompanied by a chaperone, their parent/guardian must be contacted and arrangements made for them to be taken home.
- Children are usually very excited and are worn out easily – please make allowances for this and allow them extra breaks if needed.

2.12   THINGS TO CONSIDER ON LOCATION

- Shelter needs to be available if raining.
- If it is hot, breaks need to be taken in a shaded area.
- Make the children aware of the dangers on location, e.g. on beaches and near ponds and swimming pools.
- Provide hot drinks on cold days and ensure cold drinks are available on hot days.

- Ensure the children wear any clothing they have with them that is relevant for the weather, e.g. a raincoat or sun hat.

3.   HEALTH AND SAFETY

3.1   FIRST AID AND INJURIES

- A first aider should be available at each shoot together with a complete first aid kit.
- Staff need to keep a written record of any injury that occurs, along with the treatment given. Please use the attached Child Incident Report form.

3.2   FIRE EXITS

- Children should be informed of the location of fire exits and told what to do if there is a fire alarm.
- A fire marshal must be at each shoot.

3.3   EQUIPMENT

- Children need to be made aware of the equipment around them and the dangers each piece of equipment can pose, e.g. tripping on wires, not to touch the camera etc.
- If gunge or foam has been used, then special care needs to be taken so staff and children do not slip.

3.4   TOILETS

- Toilets need to be available near to a shoot.
- Children need to be accompanied by their parent/ guardian/chaperone to the toilet.

3.5   RISK ASSESSMENT

- A risk assessment must take place before a shoot and

all risks must be explained to everyone involved before the shoot begins.

4. OTHER
4.1 DATA PROTECTION
- Children's details are not to be left on show. They MUST be locked away, and details taken on a shoot must be kept in a covered folder.
- Children's details should NEVER be disclosed to a third party.
- All freelancers working for the Photographer need to sign a declaration regarding data protection.

4.2 EQUAL OPPORTUNITIES
- Gingersnap Modelling Agency wants to give all children the same opportunities, whatever their background, age or ability.
- ALL CHILDREN MUST BE TREATED EQUALLY regardless of whether they are being paid or not.

4.3 COSTS
- Gingersnap Modelling Agency will, at their discretion, cover the cost of travel for children to/from a shoot, and of obtaining medical certificates.
- Generally, this will happen when a parent/guardian has difficulty in paying these costs, or the costs are high. Each case will be decided on an individual basis.

KEY THINGS TO REMEMBER
- Children's welfare, safety and well-being are paramount.
- Ensure all children have a licence in place before

filming.
- Obtain copies of all chaperones' licences.
- Get a signed copy of the Allergy and Medication form.
- Always complete a Child Incident Report form – even for the smallest queries or concerns.
- Don't forget, children will be children.

There are also international child licences. These are issued when children are taken out of the country to shoot abroad, and this happens a lot! International licences are much more involved, and the application must go to a magistrates' court to be granted. The documentation required is intense:
- Application form.
- Notice to Police document.
- Declaration form for children under the age of fourteen.
- An additional application form.
- The actual job contract, signed by all parties.
- A doctor's certificate stating that the child is fit to travel.
- A letter of consent from the head teacher of the child's school.
- The child's birth certificate.

International licences are issued by companies who are used to dealing with magistrates and the additional paperwork required. Do not fear – you won't be appearing in court laden with files any time soon! This will all go on behind the scenes. All you need to do as a parent is fill in the necessary forms and provide your passports.

Model agencies and clients take child licensing very seriously. The safety of all models, especially children, on shoots is a very important part of an agent's job.

Family modelling

In the world of commercial modelling, and with the onset of Covid, real family model groups have become sought after. Families and couples have a natural rapport with each other, which makes for fantastic images or footage. For the client, who covers all expenses, travel and accommodation are cheaper too, as the family will travel and stay together, so a real family model group makes great business sense to clients.

Things to consider for modelling families include:

- Do you all have regular availability?
- Can you all get to London or your nearest city for up to three castings for each job?
- Are you all prepared to do long shoots together, sometimes for days at a time?
- Are your passports in order?

Family modelling can be fun and rewarding. Not only can you spend time together, but you can also earn lots of money. Gingersnap have a family on our books who save up all their modelling money to go on lovely holidays. I think this is a great idea!

Specialist Modelling

Hand modelling

Many agencies also represent hand models. Some only deal with parts modelling, like legs, arms and hands. Advertisements featuring hands only are an important part of the modelling industry. I have been on many beauty shoots where a model's hands could not be used, and a professional hand model was matched up to the model. It might be that the beauty model's hands are not right for the shoot, or that their nails are not the right shape and size. These shoots are high budget, so every element of the imagery must be perfect. Picture a model sat in a set, with a hand model perched very close to them, using their hands to apply make-up, fix hair, or put cream on someone else's face.

Hand models should be prepared to get into all sorts of positions to do their job, and not be shy about working in close proximity to others. They are required to do many different tasks,

Cotton cools it; satin steals the limelight

Vogue Australia

119

depending on the campaign. They could be picking up a glass of wine, modelling watches or jewellery, taking a bow, making different shapes with their hands, sign language for the deaf, tying knots, cooking, writing, painting…the list goes on.

Different hand positions should be practised at home in front of a mirror. This is an important part of the role because you need to learn quickly what looks good and what doesn't. Practise with a friend, ask them to take lots of phone snaps of your hands in different positions against a pale or white wall, and have a look at the results. You'll soon learn what works. It's always best to practise holding something – a cup, a pen, maybe even a book. It's harder than you think to hold a position for a prolonged amount of time.

Clarey tip...

When your hands are pointing downwards it can create pronounced veins which don't look so pretty. Point your hands upwards and those veins magically disappear. Keep your hands pointing up in between shots!

The next stage is to book some test shoots in order to get some professional shots and to build on your experience and portfolio. Start a social media page for your hands, and follow other hand models and clients to build up your following.

In general, long, slender fingers and graceful, healthy hands with beautiful nails are the kind of hands casting directors are looking for. That's not to say that different types of hands aren't required – they are, for a variety of campaigns. Scarred, extra large or small, tattooed, hairy, or wrinkled hands, or ones with moles, can find clients to pay for pictures of them. But the work available for these types of hands will be more niche.

Hand care

Nails should be well manicured, with the flexibility to change nail shape etc. according to the brief. You should be friends with your local manicurist because, believe me, you're going to be a frequent visitor. Hand models take their craft very seriously, maintaining their hands and arms with nourishing treatments, and wearing gloves when washing up or doing household tasks to prevent scratches, scrapes or broken nails.

Once your nails are looking beautiful and you have some lovely, professional hand pictures and some experience of shooting, you can put yourself out there for work and start earning some serious money. Congratulations, you are a professional hand model!

Fitting work

Models are booked by clients for fitting work to enable the client to fit their clothes on real bodies. The work is very niche because it requires models to be a particular size and height. Weight should be kept healthy and stable as fluctuations will affect how the clothes fit.

Fitting work involves trying on clothes and samples for a client, designer or retailer. A lot of patience is necessary as the clothing is fitted onto the model's body rather than a tailor's dummy. The clothes will be measured, pinned and photographed (just digital snaps) for reference for the client and the clothing factory. You should give feedback when asked, and jump and bend to make sure the clothes work on a real body. There could be quite a few different clothes to get through, so you will need to change as swiftly as possible.

You will be required to bring a few items to every fitting session:

- Nude bra and pants/ underwear (midis for clothing fits

and thongs for lingerie fits).
- Black socks (mainly for warmth).
- Black vest to wear when doing trouser fits.
- Black shorts or big pants to wear when trying on tops.
- A book or iPad so you have something to do in downtimes.

Working as a fitting model

It is essential that you are always professional and polite. Make sure that you arrive on time. Arriving just a few minutes late can upset a client and cost them extra money if there is a lot to get through. Please make sure that you have eaten and had a drink (not alcoholic!) before you go to the session. The client will want you as 'match fit' as possible before the session starts.

You must arrive at the fitting session clean, including hair, face and nails. Please take a hairband to tie up your hair, and be sure to wear no make-up. You will be putting on and taking off clothes all day, and the last thing the client wants is make-up marks all over the clothing. Do not wear any kind of fashion or body jewellery.

Avoid eating, drinking, sitting, lying down, or smoking in the clothes you are fitting. Avoid talking about the clothes unless it is complimentary. The people fitting the clothing on you have seen these clothes through from the initial concept, so you could be inadvertently insulting the designer! You could be asked your opinion of the clothes – in these cases please remain professional at all times. You never know who is listening. If you are required to wear an outfit you do not like, or one you don't think suits you, it is not your place to comment. If you are unhappy about anything to do with the fitting session, call your agency and they will liaise with the client on your behalf.

Catwalk modelling

Fashion shows in the industry are referred to in a few different ways: Shows, runway, fashion shows, catwalk. Catwalk shows are certainly not for the faint-hearted. They are great fun, exciting and exhilarating, and there's no doubt in my mind when I say that it's the only modelling medium in which you get immediate gratification from your audience!

Show castings are crazy. There are so many models looking fabulous, all lined up waiting to see the designer and the show team. In show season there are countless back-to-back show castings. Always take a pair of heels tucked away in your bag to change into once you get to the casting.

The best way to learn how to move on the catwalk is by watching other models. The catwalk is a hotbed of talented models, as only the best walkers get booked for shows. Take advantage and keep your sisters and brothers close! Walking properly takes time and patience. You need to practise regularly in front of a full-length mirror. Everyone has their own walking style and rhythm, so embrace your style. Once I took a brilliant show director out for a coffee and asked him how models could walk like supermodels. He said there were three key things to consider:

1. Walk like you're on a tightrope: one foot in front of the other.
2. Practise walking with something like an umbrella behind your arms and across your back in order to keep your back straight.
3. Imagine you have a piece of string pulling you up from the top of your head. Keep that head high and straight, baby!

Each show has its own brief regarding the vibe. You will be told in rehearsal what is required. I have done the lot! Smiling and bouncy, straight-faced and straight-bodied with no hips, sexy and flirty…the list goes on.

Practice makes perfect!

At home, look in a mirror, try to hold your mouth naturally, and observe how that feels. Hold your lips together without forcing them closed or open. Keep your eyes focused on a point straight ahead of you. Do not look around the room – stay focused. Look alert and walk with purpose – this should show in your eyes and face. Don't make eye contact with anyone in the audience; try to keep your gaze fixed straight ahead. Hold your body straight and tall, and as you strut forward, project confidence. Let your hips move in a more exaggerated way without overdoing it. Allow your arms to hang at your sides and keep your hands relaxed, swinging very slightly with your body's movement. Practise walking in your heels, as they will automatically give you more height and sass. Play music and keep your step constant with the rhythm whilst sustaining your forward gaze. Think supermodel energy!

There is a lot to think about and it will take you a while to get your vibe going. Remember to do your research. Thanks to the proliferation of videos on YouTube, you can watch the masters at work. Naomi Campbell remains the Queen of the Catwalk, but also look at the predatorial strut of Karlie Kloss. Kate Moss has

Practice that look in the mirror!
Photographer Sarah Maingot

a more bouncy, casual style, while Sasha Pivovarova's walk is gentler and more determined and composed. For confidence boosts, watch Victoria's Secret shows. They are fun, sexy and aesthetically pleasing. No harm at all in imagining yourself up there with those angels!

Male models, you should be looking to walk naturally like you are walking along the street with a little more swagger than usual. Hold your head up and be proud. Your turn should be cool and slow to allow the audience to see a 360-degree view of your whole outfit. There will be a briefing before the show or casting. Listen to the instructions. The best directors will physically show you what they want and will correct you as you walk.

Male Modelling

Male model David Gandy from Essex (born 19 February 1980) is an English fashion model who began his career after winning a televised model-search competition. David is one of the most successful male models of our time, heading up campaigns for a variety of companies including Marks & Spencer, Hugo Boss, Massimo Dutti, Russell & Bromley and Dolce & Gabbana.

There's no doubt that David is a one-off in the male modelling world because he's a household name.

So – how did he do it?

Well, timing for one. For years it seemed that more slightly-built male models were sought after. Then, in 2001, Gandy hit the scene with his broad shoulders and muscles; he changed the narrative for male models. In 2008, photographer Mario Testino shot Gandy for Dolce & Gabbana's fragrance shoot 'Light Blue'. Gandy was displayed on 50-foot billboards in Times Square and, with 11 million hits online, he became a household name around the globe. A hard act to follow!

According to the <u>National Centre for Biotechnology</u>

Information, the world supply of women's clothing is at least seven times larger than that of men's clothing. These statistics alone demonstrate how much tougher male modelling is than the dominating womenswear industry is for female models. Young male models starting out have more competition for the limited jobs available, and I would say that it's much harder to make money.

But do not despair! Clarey is here to guide you towards the best way to succeed as male model:

1. **Dress well.** Have a staple of five to ten pieces which can be changed according to the casting. Keep a bank of plain T-shirts in your wardrobe, a few pairs of smart trousers and jeans. Always have a well-tailored suit. High street stores are great; just make sure the suit fits you beautifully. Always own a good pair of leather shoes – shoes maketh the man! Choose carefully. Remember, if you look good, you feel good, and if you feel great, you'll get that job nailed.

2. **Hair.** Make sure your hair is nicely cut and clean. Facial hair should be fitting to the job or casting you are going for. If the shoot brief is for clean-shaven, go clean-cut as if you have the job already. If you are not sure, and have stubble, take your shaving kit with you so you're prepared.

3. **Hygiene.** You could very well be working closely with other models. Take a small bag with deodorant, moisturising cream, and a good lip balm as well as that shaving kit.

4. **Mentality.** Be confident and positive. In this book, I have talked a lot about the logistics of getting booked on jobs. Confidence *without arrogance* is key here, and there is a fine line! Go in as if you already have the

job, smile and use the clients name – they will notice. Remember to give them your model card and repeat your name so you'll be remembered.

Editorial modelling

Editorials are shoots for magazines; either online or paper ones. They are four- to ten-page visual stories that showcase trends, fashion, beauty and lifestyle. Hair, make-up and props feature heavily in editorial shoots.

Models should aspire to do editorial shoots because they are often full-page bleeds, which are great for models' portfolios. A 'full-page bleed' is an image which covers the whole page from edge to edge. It's no mistake that the size of a regular magazine is roughly the same size as your physical portfolio. Because many editorial shoots happen daily, they will earn you less money than advertising and commercial shoots. When I was nineteen, I was booked for my first job for *Vogue*. I was so pleased. Then I was told the fee: £50![18] I was more than surprised. Why so low for such a high-end magazine? Well, there are a couple of things at work here. Firstly, being booked for *Vogue* is still an honour in this

Vogue Australia

18   I believe the *Vogue* fee has gone up since then, but it will still just cover your expenses.

Sky Magazine,
photographer Derek Henderson

industry. Times change, but being shot for *Vogue* will always be a standout moment, and you are guaranteed to be working with an amazing team. Secondly, if you have a full bleed from *Vogue* in your book, You. Are. Guaranteed. More. Work. That is just how it works. Advertising clients will see the pictures and want to work with you. It's that simple.

Editorial clients seek an edgier look depending on the story they are creating. The style of an editorial model is more creative to fit with the story you are telling. There will be a brief at the start of the shoot. You will be involved when the editorial staff plan your hair and make-up first thing in the morning. Always take your portfolio, because the team will want to refer to your pictures – you have been booked for this job because of the look you portray in your book. Typically, in editorial shoots there are separate hair and make-up teams involved, because each element is very involved and key to the look. Be open-minded! You could be working at the heart of cutting-edge fashion, so go with the flow. The professionals surrounding you are experts in their field; they will know what they want!

Remember that the day of the shoot is one of the end results of weeks of planning. You are part of the creative process. I remember doing a shoot for *Tatler* in which they didn't want to put mascara on my very pale eyelashes. I was mortified because my eyes are small anyway, so without pronounced lashes they appear completely lost. Do not fear and do not complain. The hair and make-up team are working to the brief.

Be prepared to offer a quirkier modelling style. Editorial teams are after various angles incorporating your whole body. They may want extreme facial expressions, or for you to remain static, or run and jump whilst holding different expressions. The photographic team will liaise with you throughout the day to clarify what's expected. These days are super creative, requiring input from all members of the team, including you. Do not be scared to input ideas yourself. The best editorial days are so much fun because they feel like a team effort from all sides. The shoot could very well develop into one which wasn't necessarily planned at the beginning of the day. I once did an editorial in Germany for which I arrived impossibly tired. They caught my vibe early on and had me lying on a bed for the duration of the shoot – that really worked for me and for the shoot, but I am convinced that they didn't plan it; it was just how things panned out for the look on the day. Be flexible. Things could very well change throughout the shoot. At another editorial shoot there happened to be a beautiful dog in the next studio – guess who appeared in the magazine with the dog?

It's not all glamour, though. Editorial modelling is not as easy as it looks. Whether you are on location or in a studio, be prepared to hold your body in uncomfortable positions for hours on end. Don't forget that you will be modelling trends for the following summer during the winter, and vice versa, so you are always either boiling hot or freezing cold. There is no happy medium in modelling, I'm afraid to say. Just don't complain, because you want to get booked again. Gossip concerning complaining and moaning models travels fast in the industry. People love a good chat at shoots, and everyone is all ears. Always be a pro.

Commercial modelling

Commercial modelling is the industry's largest area because it covers so many different things: lingerie, advertising, sports, hair products, catalogues, print ads, product packaging, online, social media, point-of-sale advertising and countless others. Shoots involve both moving images and stills. If you are on a stills shoot, there will often be a film crew filming behind-the-scenes footage to use on social media.

Commercial modelling can be very lucrative. TV and cinema advertising pay a huge amount depending on where the ad will be aired worldwide. Billboards and other 'out-of-home' advertising can also pay very well. Always clarify with your agent (or the client if you don't have an agent) before the job what the usage for the shoot will be, as this very much determines your fee.

Things have certainly changed in the past few years in terms of commercial modelling. Fashion model agencies used to be very clear about the distinction between commercial and fashion models. Historically, female fashion models were over five foot nine and size eight to ten, which are the sample sizes for the designers and brands who make up the bulk of their clients. Fashion models have strong, distinctive features: sharp cheekbones, long necks and elongated limbs. Commercial models vary in height and body shape, but always have a great, toothy smile and a more accessible 'girl next door' vibe. Over the years, however, the lines between fashion and commercial models have become blurred, so more commercial models have been taken on by fashion agencies and vice versa. Money talks, and commercial models make money, so the industry has been led by the market.

Fashion model Rosie Huntington-Whiteley explained this shift in an interview with Ashley Graham: "Social media just started coming into play, and girls that would be considered to be commercial had much more approachability. It was just that a consumer, or an audience, related more with commercial models, and so the industry would see these girls' followers and their audience was much bigger, and something happened where you would start to see other women – you know, kind of high fashion – walking down the runway, and suddenly, we were embraced in a different way."[19]

The requirements for commercial modelling are much more fluid than they are for fashion modelling. Height and size are not as important: the obsession with female models being five foot ten is relaxed, meaning those who are five foot five or even smaller will be considered. Size eight becomes size ten to sixteen, depending on the client's needs. Contrary to popular belief, many successful commercial models look like normal, everyday girls or the guy next door. Whatever a model's size or height, a great smile is essential!

Successful commercial models are set apart by their ability to replicate various looks, time and time again, on demand. Actors often cross over into commercial modelling, aided by their training in projecting different looks and personalities. Good commercial models are very photogenic and can have a beautiful, generic or unique look. The demand for new commercial models is very high, with many companies competing for the most exciting and memorable models who best represent their brand.

---

19   Rosie Huntington-Whiteley, *Pretty Big Deal with Ashley Graham*, 3 December 2019.

My own agency, Gingersnap, is a commercial model agency. When people ask me, "What makes a model?", I always reply, "The person who can sell a stick of chewing gum, a can of Coke, a vacuum cleaner, a supermarket, a pair of shoes...you name it, they will be able to sell everyday products to everyday customers."

E-commerce modelling

E-commerce or e-comm modelling comes under the branch of commercial modelling. It is a huge industry involving a very different kind of modelling. Most clothes are sold online as well as in stores. E-comm clients photograph hundreds of items of clothing every week. Models are between five foot six and five foot eight for women, and five foot eleven and six foot for men.

E-comm clients have certain poses to which models should adhere throughout the day, and there are generally around fifteen to sixty different outfits to get through. The days are long and taxing, and models need to be forever on the ball. If your first booking goes well, this work is constant and lucrative, and you will be rebooked.

E-comm jobs are known in the trade as 'bread-and-butter jobs'. These constant bookings pay the rent when other paid jobs are scarce. E-comm work has overtaken the catalogue jobs of the past, as the 'fast fashion' industry has taken hold quickly, especially in the wake of the pandemic.

Social Media

Social media platforms have become essential tools for building a model's brand. Many agencies encourage models to have a social media following because it boosts work opportunities. I recommend that my models maintain two accounts on each major platform: one for their personal life and the other for their professional work. The professional accounts should show not only your portfolio, but also behind-the-scenes (BTS) and personality posts, such as ones about travel, make-up and photography.

What's your vibe?

You build your followers on social media sites like Instagram by posting funny, inspirational or relatable content which your followers will enjoy. Your vibe attracts your tribe and gradually expands your follower count. Write a great bio which tells followers why they should follow you. Don't forget to add your agency details or your own contact details, so potential clients know who to get hold of when the bookings come flooding in.

Next, create a posting plan. The social media management client Later[20] comes in handy here, as it allows you to schedule posts even when you're working, and shows you detailed insights into who's viewing your posts.

Remember to use hashtags to attract your audience. Some ideas are:

---

20   https://later.com/

- #modeling
- #modelling
- #fashionmodel
- #commercialmodelling
- #behindthescenes
- #BTS
- #modellife
- #soyouwanttobeamodel

Why not even start your own hashtag? I started #thesecretlifeofmodels to launch this book! This way, there aren't millions of posts under the same generic hashtag.

Words of warning

Don't post excessive bad language or inappropriate pictures, debate controversial topics, or share extreme and potentially offensive views which could damage your career in the long run. Inappropriate posts have a horrible habit of kicking celebrities in the ass years down the line. You never know where your career will take you, so get into the habit of practising good social media etiquette now.

Make sure your settings are adjusted so that you can approve all images and videos in which you are tagged.

Another important point is your health and safety. Models are like magnets on social media platforms. You will build your following fast, but alongside the good followers, there will be questionable ones with, perhaps, the wrong intentions. Common sense should always prevail when it comes to unsavoury characters. Keep those baddies out of your DMs! Do not arrange to meet anyone or book any job without talking it through with your agency. If you do not have an agency, do your due diligence and all your checks to find out if the job is kosher.

If there is any doubt, and things sound like they're too good to be true, it's guaranteed that they *are* too good to be true and there will be a catch. Never put yourself at risk.

A golden rule is to engage with your audience regularly. Be interactive and interesting. Ask your followers for their opinions. Use polls, question stickers and music to make posts look and feel fabulous. Tag everyone involved in the shoot: photographer, make-up artist, stylist and client. Don't hold back from tagging the brands and people you want to collaborate with. It will get you noticed faster and lead like-minded followers straight to you. Collaborate with colleagues who boost your brand – especially if they have a larger following than you. Interview, mention and tag each other.

Always be positive and happy, because everyone loves a great story. It will widen your reach and grow your tribe. Follow the models and clients you look up to and the brands you aspire to. Don't get hung up on posts looking overly perfect, overly filtered and over the top. Be real with your vibe to enable your followers to get a sense of the real you! Be brave, be insightful, be a trailblazer and you will soon be noticed.

Inclusivity and Diversity in the Modelling World

The subject of inclusivity and diversity is one that is very close to my heart, and one which has underpinned my whole career, from model to agent, so it's only right to spend some time diving into this key topic. I started this journey championing the rebellion against the idea of size zero models, and this is where I am going to end. I believe that the modelling industry has a place for anyone who wants to enter it, and that today it is a far kinder and more inclusive place than it was when I first walked through its doors all those years ago. Let me illuminate the entrance sign for you...

Supermodel Naomi Campbell was one of the first campaigners to speak out about the representation of models of colour within the fashion industry. In a *Channel 4 News* interview she spoke about writing to designers, stylists, magazines and casting directors to ask them to consider a fair balance of black and white models: "I am saying that the act of not choosing models of colour is racist... We don't want them to hide behind aesthetics, we want them to allow balance diversity... just be aware."[21] This was in 2013, when Naomi felt that the fashion industry was more concerned about the look and feel of campaigns than it was about equality. This interview is nearly ten years old now, and, thanks to people like Naomi using their

---

21   Naomi Campbell, *Channel 4 News*, 16 September 2013.

status to speak out, there has been a definite representational shift within the industry.

In 2014, Ivo Raspudic, a fifty-one-year-old mechanical engineer, was scouted at a party. In a 2021 interview with *Vogue* he spoke about the importance of diversity, stating, "People need someone to look up to in any industry, no matter your age. I have people tell me how great it is for them to see someone in their age group doing what I do, wearing what I wear. It's nice to know that it sends a message of inclusivity – that fashion is for everyone."[22] Ivo found himself being booked for both campaigns and catwalk shows, and designers chose to buck the trend of booking five-foot-ten-plus, mainly white male models, to instead showcase a carousel of models who were diverse in terms of ethnicity, size, age and disability.

Today, people like Winnie Harlow, the Jamaican-Canadian fashion model who has the skin condition vitiligo, have found their way onto the covers of *Elle*, *Vogue*, *Harpers* and *Glamour*. Differences have been embraced, barriers have been broken down, and beauty has been redefined for a new age. This is a huge step forward for an industry that was for decades dominated by waiflike white supermodels. Fashion models no longer belong to an exclusive club; diverse models are taken on by agencies. They are unapologetically themselves – unparalleled and fabulously individual. In turn, advertisers have embraced the different and the trailblazers, helping to break down conventional barriers to get their brands into the limelight. All of these new talents have had the opportunity to use their individuality to create a niche for themselves, and some have even been able to build a successful brand around their unique features.

To a lesser extent, I experienced a similar situation in the '90s. As a red-headed model, I was always placed in casting

22   Ivo Raspudic, *Vogue*, 24 January 2021.

rooms and pictures with other models who were just 'different'. We were 'the others', brought in because we represented the mainstream minority. Often, you'd hear the bookers shout across the booking desk, "They want blonde or brunette only… no redheads!" There was just an acceptance that redheads represented a niche market and were wheeled in when ethereal, Scottish- or Irish-looking models were in the brief. "You don't need any eye make-up – we'll just put some blusher on you," clients would say, time after time. It worked in my favour, though. When clients wanted a red-headed model, there were only about three of us in the whole industry! We all cleaned up, so if you can find your niche, work to your strengths. Every now and again, I got a shoot where they piled on the make-up and lit me up like a Christmas tree and I was in my element. I loved those shoots because it was so different from my usual ethereal fairy vibe.

Agencies have sprung up to promote equality and diversity within the fashion, beauty and media industries. People of minority – including larger and petite models, disabled people and non-binary people – are being represented. Everyone who wants to can take their rightful place in the limelight. That place has been carved out for them by previous diverse models, like Winnie Harlow and Naomi Campbell, who battled to the top. The growth of diversity is undeniable.

Conclusion

What makes a great model?

I thought this would be useful: I sat some industry experts down and asked them what they think the keys are to being a successful model. Here are their pointers:

- Have confidence and believe in yourself.
- Say 'yes' to most things your agent puts you forward for. They are managing your career and know your market.
- Treat it like a business, always be professional and nice, and be prepared for anything.
- Be yourself.

Well, there you have it! My life and world in nearly 35,000 words. I really hope that it offers you some valuable insights into the world of modelling, and provides a window into how this fabulous thing works, from humble beginnings of initial tests to the magazine shelves, film sets and screen. I have taken you through every aspect of the modelling world, a world that is deeply ingrained

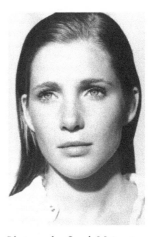

Photographer Sarah Maingot

in my soul, which I now very gladly impart to you. Hopefully I have answered some questions you may have long pondered. If you are inspired by this wonderful industry, please step inside my office and ask more questions. I'm more than happy to share.

The model industry has been my life for the past thirty years. It's given me some magical, memorable and unforgettable experiences – all of which could never fit within the pages of this book. I've encountered some incredible highs and some dramatic lows; as we all do in life. It's not all glamour. Not everyone gets to be the next Cindy Crawford, Gisele Bündchen or Bella Hadid. But it is fulfilling and, if you're prepared to work hard, incredibly rewarding. Over the past thirty years, the industry has transformed into a more honest, open, tolerant and inclusive place. I'm happy to say that one day, I'll be leaving the industry satisfied that it is now a kinder place than I once found it. If you take anything from this book, let it be this. You do not have to be five foot ten and a size zero bombshell to be in this world. There is room for everyone – yes, even you.

Now, let's get to work!

Appendix

Clarey's A–Z of Modelling

Above the line

Above-the-line marketing involves using mass media methods to target a large number of consumers. Media channels include television advertising, radio and billboards. Above-the-line usage pays well, as the reach is far wider than it is for below-the-line usage. In filming terms, 'above the line' refers to the hierarchy of the team on a film set, with the directors and producers at the top and the assistants at the bottom.

Accounts

An agency's accounts department deals with invoicing and money. You could also come across an 'account handler' – that's a client with whom you might have a casting.

Advance

Sometimes a model needs her/his money early. This is possible – ask your agency, but bear in mind that you will be charged a fee to get your cash early. It may not be possible if you're a new client for your agency, but fingers crossed. If in doubt, ask the accounts department.

Advertising/advertisement
Advertising is a marketing tactic involving paying for space to promote a product, service or cause. These promotional messages are called advertisements, or 'ads' for short. The goal of advertising is to reach the people most likely to pay for a company's products or services and entice them to buy. Model agencies will negotiate a larger fee for advertising depending on the global or national spread and the time limit of the images or footage.

Advertorial
This means that images will appear in a magazine once for a particular (usually high-street) company. It's like a one-off advertisement, and pays more than editorial (magazine) rates.

Agency
Your key to getting work! Check out the 'Agencies' chapter for more info.

Art director
The person on a shoot who has created and is responsible for the look of the final images. They look at every element and bring them together to produce the finished piece.

Assistant
This is a word you will hear a lot in this industry. There are assistants for every role: director, producer, make-up, stylist, digital... Like you, assistants are learning about the business, so be super nice to them.

Availability

One of the most important questions you will be asked as a model is, "Are you available?" Your answer needs to be a 'yes' or a 'no', and you need to be flexible. One of the best attributes of a good model is having a handle on your own schedule. Availability means bookings, and the quicker you get back to your agency on your availability, the more likely they are to put you forward for a job. Keep a diary so that you will instantly know your availability at any given time. There are some great diary apps available for most smartphones.

Basic studio fee (BSF)

The fee you get for a photo session.

Beauty shoot

Clean shots with perfect make-up and hair, and no gimmicks hiding your cheekbones or skin. Just you. You'll need a great beauty shoot for your book.

Behind the scenes (BTS)

Behind-the-scenes shots are great for using on social media. These shots document things like having your make-up and hair done, being dressed and other fun that goes on behind the scenes. Much like this book, BTS shots offer a rare glimpse into the inner workings on set, and are a great opportunity to show all your Instagram followers how fun your job can be!

Below the line

Below-the-line marketing is a more direct and targeted form of advertising that can often be found on social media. The main thing to remember with usage is how many people are going to see it. If it's below the line, the audience is smaller than for above-the-line campaigns, and this will usually be reflected in the fee.

Billboard
Billboards are typically placed in high-traffic areas, such as along highways and in cities, so they are seen by the highest number of drivers and pedestrians. Billboard advertising is effective for building brand awareness to as many people as possible.

Book
Another word for a portfolio.

Booked
You've got a job! Good work.

Booker
Your bookers should be your best friends: they make up your agency and push you to clients, arrange your jobs and control your bookings. They are the key to getting booked. Make friends with them, buy them doughnuts, and it will pay off.

Book out
If you're unavailable for a long period of time for whatever reason – it could be a holiday, or a big job with another agency – you'll need to be booked out. Communication is key here: your agency needs to know if you're out of the country so they don't put you forward to clients while you're away. Another reason to keep a diary!

Brief
An initial visual and/or written statement of the final image or film.

Buyout

Essentially, an advanced payment on the future use of the photos from a job. The size of a buyout depends on where the pictures will be used, how long they will be used for, and whether the campaign is above or below the line. Buyouts can be extended when the initial buyout has expired, and that usually means another sum of money. They can be the gift that keeps on giving.

Callback

When the client's team want to see you again after an initial casting. It means you've impressed them! You can sometimes get paid for callbacks, so check with your agency.

Call sheet

The job bible. A document that tells you where you need to be and when, who to call if things go wrong, and what can be expected from a shoot. You should get a call sheet for each job or test.

Call time

The time when you need to arrive at a shoot to start hair and make-up. Don't be late.

Camera operator

The Camera operator is the person responsible for setting up the camera equipment and capturing the director's shots

Casting

A kind of interview for a job. Even though a client or casting director will have seen your book, they may need to meet you in person to check out your current look. See the 'Be That Model' chapter for tips.

Casting director/agent

The person in charge of finding the right model, actor or presenter for the brief. They liaise directly with agencies and artists.

Chaperone

A person who takes care of a child at a shoot. A government-licensed individual who is appointed and paid to protect working children. A parent can be the legal chaperone for their own child, as long as they are not modelling too.

Chart

Another name for 'diary'. Your chart displays all your jobs, castings and tests. If you have a mother agency, they might hold and control your chart for you.

Client

Anyone can be a client, from a massive multinational company to a small boutique, or even a one-man band. A happy shoot makes for a happy client, which means more bookings.

Commercial

As a noun, a TV advert. As an adjective, an engagement with commercial gain (i.e. one that makes money). See the commercial modelling section of the 'Specialist Modelling' chapter for more information.

Comp card/comp

A model's business card.

Confirmed/confirmation

If you've been confirmed for a job, you've got it! Put it in your diary!

Contract

Your contract with an agency is very important: it tells you their terms, their commission and everything you need to know about being represented by them. Any contract you sign, you will need to keep, in case you need to refer to anything later.

Day rate/fee

How much you are getting paid per day, half-day or hour of shooting. This can also be called the basic studio fee (BSF). Essentially, your payment for shooting. Usage is paid on top of the day rate.

Digital

This typically refers to digital footage and images.

Digitals

Instant snaps of a model, usually wearing little make-up.

Digital team

The crew in charge of digital film capture.

Director

In the film industry, the person responsible for bringing the story to life on screen.

Director of photography

The person responsible for translating the script into a visual image.

E-commerce/e-comm

Business transactions conducted on the internet. Basically, internet sales; a huge part of modelling work today.

Edgy
At the forefront of a trend, experimental or avant-garde.

Editorial
Media content which contains news, information or comment rather than advertising. For a model, it's great to do a lot of editorial shoots as your portfolio is soon brought up to date.

Expenses
For jobs with a bigger budget, expenses are almost always covered. This can include your travel to and from the shoot, your food throughout the day, or any other costs associated with shooting. Always, always, always keep receipts for expenses, so your agent can invoice the client for them.

Featured
If you are featured, this means that you will be fully recognisable and highlighted in the final edit.

Featured extra
As with 'featured', but there are other extras around you who could also be fully recognisable and highlighted in the final edit.

Fee
The lump sum you're paid for a job. Usually made up of a basic studio fee, usage and expenses. You should always know your fee before a job takes place.

First option
You have been put on a hold, or heavy-pencilled for a job. This should not be superseded by any other appointment.

Fitting

A session with the stylist before a big shoot, in which you try on clothes. This is usually paid.

Fitting work or job

When a client needs a model of a particular size to try on clothes, shoes or underwear to check that they have all been made to the correct size. It is usually paid by the hour, or sometimes a day fee is applicable, depending on how much the client has to get through.

Flesh-coloured underwear

An absolute necessity. You need a great set (or two) of nude underwear. It is advisable to wear nude underwear to every test or job, as it is discreet under lots of different types of clothes. Strapless bras are often requested too, so you should invest in some basic 'work' underwear.

Global

Worldwide. In modelling terms, this refers to where in the world campaign footage or images are displayed.

Grips

The lighting and rigging technicians who are responsible for all the lighting and camera equipment rigged over the cast and crew. There are several roles for grips:

- **Key grip** is in charge of the grip department.
- **Best boy grip** assists the key grip and oversees the rental of equipment on set.
- **Dolly grip** operates the camera cranes and wheeled carts holding the camera.
- **Gaffer** is the head of the electrical department.
- **Best boy electric** assists the gaffer and is responsible

for the daily running of the lighting, and hiring and scheduling of the crew.

Hair and make-up
Your day starts with this, usually with a coffee in hand. Early-morning hair and make-up is the first step of a job. There will be make-up and hair on most jobs. Arrive with a clean face and clean hair, and let them know if you're allergic to anything. In some cases where there are minimal requirements, or on a test shoot, you might be asked to do your own hair and make-up. If so, your agency will advise you of this in advance. For every job you do, you must ask your agency if there is hair and make-up.

Health and Safety
The film location should fit into the correct government guidelines so that no harm is caused to models, artists and crew throughout the duration of the shoot.

Heavy pencil
See 'first option'. The client is very keen on you and has first refusal on you.

HMUA
Hair-and-make-up artist.

Internal usage
Images used on a business-to-business basis only. The usage payment for internal usage might not be as high as for billboards, for example.

Job
A shoot/job day.

Kids' board/table

The bookers who work on children's bookings.

Lighting

The lights used to light up the set or shooting area.

Loader

Responsible for the actual film on a film set.

Location

The site where the shoot is taking place.

Location manager

The person responsible for the location on the shoot day. This person obtains all necessary licences and permissions for the shoot day so that all the paperwork is in order. The location manager also makes sure that the location is both fit for filming (in terms of health and safety) and looked after throughout the shoot days.

Location scout

The person responsible for finding the shoot/film location.

Location van

The van which takes models to a location and stays there for the whole shoot day. Models change and have their hair and make-up done in the location van. The nicest ones have a kitchen, a bathroom and a chill-out area.

Main board

The bookers who book an agency's main male and female models.

Manicure

A cosmetic treatment of hands involving shaping and often painting of the nails, removal of cuticles and softening of the skin. Sometimes models are required to get a manicure before a shoot.

Men's board/table

The male-model booking team in a model agency.

Model card

A model's business card, left with a client after a casting. It usually contains a main headshot, four different shots, the model's measurements and the agency's contact details.

Mother agency

A model's main agency. The mother agency talks to all other agencies around the world and other cities who also represent that model, and holds the model's diary so that there is only one point of contact for the model.

Mood Board

A mood board is a compilation of images which project the shoot's concept.

MUA

Make-up artist.

National

Usually refers to the usage of imagery or footage within your country.

New faces

New and fresh models to the modelling industry.

Non-exclusive
A model who is not attached to any particular agency or client.

Option
A pencil or hold on a date and/or model.

Option off
A pencil or hold on a date and/or model has been released.

Out of home (OOH)
Out-of-home advertising is any billboard or digital screen displayed at street level. Mostly referred to regarding the usage of imagery.

Pedicure
Professional maintenance of the nails and skin of the feet. Sometimes this is required by clients for shoots.

Pencil
A hold on a date (or dates).

Per diem
Expenses paid in cash by the client for an evening meal or other expenses when models are shooting jobs. When models are shooting for a number of days, the client is responsible for all meals. It is sometimes the client's choice to give cash called *per diem* for this purpose.

Photographer
The person who is taking the stills shots behind the camera.

Photoshop

A computer software program for editing images.

Pitch

At this stage, the job is an idea which is being presented to a client by a prospective team. Pitches are mostly paid, but sometimes treated as a test. It's great for a model to do a pitch because the client could love it and book you for the actual shoot or – even better – use the images or footage they already have, in which case you get a usage fee. You also get to meet a new team who might book you for other work for other clients, so it's win-win.

Point of sale (POS)

Images placed next to a product being sold in a shop. POS usually means more money for the model.

Polaroids

Originally pictures from an actual Polaroid camera, now these are digital images from a smartphone or camera. All good agencies take digitals, mostly with the model wearing little or no make-up so that clients can see what they look like. These could be headshots, body shots, full-length or three-quarter shots from all angles. It's great if your agency holds a set of good digitals of you, as this can sometimes reduce the time you spend attending castings.

Portfolio

Also known as a book. A selection of a model's best and most up-to-date images. Keep it clean and carry it around with you to jobs and tests.

Print

In terms of usage, this could be newspapers, magazines, flyers, postcards…anything that is printed with ink.

Producer
An individual who plans a shoot and books all the artists, studios, locations etc. They negotiate all the costs and are in charge of the whole budget.

Production team
In stills photography, the whole creative team (photographer, assistant, make-up artist, stylist…). In filming, production team refers to the creative team too (producer, director, screenwriter, art director, costume designer, cinematographer, editor…).

Public relations (PR)
In terms of the usage of pictures, PR images might be used anywhere in a magazine or newspaper for a one-off article about the product, place, clothing etc. you are modelling.

Publish
Prepare and issue (a book, journal, piece of music etc.) for public sale.

Recognisable
If you are recognised in the final edit, you are identifiable as you in the shot/final edit. This could be important in terms of your fee as a model (i.e. unrecognisable isn't as lucrative).

Regional
Regional usage means that the imagery or footage will be displayed in particular towns or cities only.

Release
The pencil/option has been released, has come off, has been let go or cancelled. Learn to love 'no'! It's okay; you'll get the next one. You can't book every job.

Representation/representing
To be entitled or appointed to act or speak for someone, especially in an official capacity.

Scout
A person with connections to model agencies who identifies people's modelling potential. Model scouts are all over the place!

Scrim
A piece of fabric in a frame which shades a shooting area.

Second option
A second pencil for a job, meaning that you already have a first option. A second option is superseded by a first option, but not by any other option after that.

Shoot/shoot day
The day the images are taken.

Show
A fashion show.

Social media
Websites and applications designed to allow people to share content quickly, efficiently and in real time. Many people define social media as apps on their smartphone or tablet. Sometimes referred to as 'social'.

Stats

Statistics or measurements.

Stills

Static photographs as opposed to a motion picture.

Street casting

Some jobs require casting agents to go out on the street and cast people for shoots. This happens a lot in big cities, so watch out for the agents with their cameras and clipboards, accosting anyone who fits their brief.

Studio

The room where all the action happens.

Styling/stylist

The person on and behind set who deals with all aspects of the clothing. Styling is referred to as 'styling' the clothing on a shoot.

Team

The group of people on a shoot.

Tear sheet

Full-bleed pictures in a magazine which can be torn out (very carefully!) at the spine and put in a portfolio.

Test

A shoot with no money involved.

Time for print (TFP)

Testing for images.

Travel day

The day a model travels to a shoot. This usually counts as paid time.

Travel expenses/fee

The fee paid to the model to cover the travel expenses.

TVC

Television commercial.

Unrec

This word is the shortened version of *unrecognisable*. *Unrec* shoots are not as lucrative as *Recognisable* shoots. Unrec means you cannot be identifiable as you in the final cut.

Usage

Where the images or footage will be used and for how long. The model should know this information before they do the shoot so that they know what they have signed up for.

Virtual casting

A casting carried out via an online platform such as Zoom when a model or artist can't be there in person.

VO

Voice-over.

VOA

Voice-over artist.

Women's board/table

The female-model booking team in a model agency.

Z card

A model card.

Credits

Audiovisual

Pretty Big Deal with Ashley Graham, Rosie Huntington-Whiteley interview, 3 December 2019

This Morning, Cara Delevingne interview, 9 October 2017

Photographers

Derek Henderson

Nick Otley

Sarah Maingot

Steve Shaw

Thomas Krygier

Print

British Fashion Council, *Fashioning a Healthy Future: The Report of the Model Health Inquiry*, September 2007

Cosmopolitan magazine (Australia)

Vogue magazine (Australia)

Sky magazine (United Kingdom)

Mode magazine (Australia)

Websites
GOV.UK: https://www.gov.uk/

Junior magazine: https://www.juniormagazine.co.uk/

Vogue magazine: https://www.vogue.co.uk/

With a little help from my friends...

Damion, my husband and saviour
Amber, my daughter who championed this book
from the beginning
Darcy, my beautiful voice of reason
Connie, my little angel
Yasmin and my amazing Gingersnap team past and present
Jim Butler, the amazing editor
Helen Hart, who brought this book to life

Lightning Source UK Ltd.
Milton Keynes UK
UKHW031041240123
415879UK00004B/341